FUTURE CITIES

Exploring Tomorrow's

Urban Landscapes and

Eco-Friendly Living

OSMAN KARAKAS

About Book

Book Title: Future Cities

Exploring Tomorrow's Urban Landscapes and Eco-Friendly Living

Type: Digital E-Book

Format: Word/PDF

Size: 6X9 inches - 15.24X22.89 cm

Total Pages: **161**

E-mail: okarakas@hotmail.com

Web: www.osmankarakas.com

CONTENTS

Preface:

Welcome to the future, where the boundaries of imagination meet the realities of urban transformation. In the pages of this book, we embark on a captivating journey through the very essence of our cities, exploring not just the structures of steel and concrete, but the vibrant communities and sustainable living that define them.

Future Cities: Exploring Tomorrow's Urban Landscapes and Eco-Friendly Living is a testament to the visionary concepts and real-life implementations shaping the cities of our dreams. In an era where the global population is increasingly urban, understanding the intricate dynamics of urban living becomes paramount. This book seeks to unravel the mysteries of urbanization, taking you through the evolution of cities from ancient settlements to the cutting-edge metropolises of tomorrow.

We dive deep into the heart of urban planning, discussing sustainable architecture, renewable energy solutions, waste management innovations, and advanced technologies that are reshaping our cities into eco-friendly havens.

From the buzz of autonomous vehicles to the tranquility of green spaces, we explore every facet of urban life, emphasizing the harmony between human habitation and the natural world.

Throughout these pages, you will encounter the challenges and triumphs of modern cities. From earthquake-resistant buildings to smart grids, from community-driven initiatives to data-driven decision-making, we present a comprehensive view of cities as living, breathing entities, constantly evolving and adapting.

But this book is more than a mere exploration of structures and systems; it is a celebration of human ingenuity and the collective drive to create a better tomorrow. It delves into the minds of architects, engineers, and innovators, showcasing their groundbreaking ideas that promise a future where urban living is not just sustainable but delightful.

As you turn the pages, envision the skylines of the future, where green roofs stretch towards the heavens, where transportation is not just efficient but environmentally conscious, and where every drop of water is cherished. Imagine a city where technology serves humanity, where communities thrive, and where the concept of waste is but a distant memory.

Future Cities is not just a book; it's a call to action. It challenges us to rethink our cities, to reimagine our urban spaces, and to believe in the transformative power of sustainable living. Whether you are an urban planner, an environmental enthusiast, or simply a curious reader, this book invites you to explore the limitless possibilities of our future cities.

So, let's embark on this journey together, where the present meets the future, and where the cities of our dreams become the cities of our reality.

Welcome to the future. Welcome to Future Cities.

Introduction

In the heart of the modern world, where cities pulse with life and innovation, a new era of urban living is dawning. Our planet is witnessing an unprecedented shift: more people than ever before are choosing to make cities their home. As this urban landscape expands, it brings forth both challenges and opportunities. How do we create cities that are not just concrete jungles but thriving ecosystems where humanity and nature coexist harmoniously? How can we transform urban spaces into vibrant, sustainable havens for all?

Future Cities: Exploring Tomorrow's Urban Landscapes and Eco-Friendly Living is a compelling exploration of the future that awaits us. In the chapters that follow, we embark on a visionary journey through the very essence of urban evolution. This book is not just a compilation of facts and figures; it's a tapestry woven from the threads of innovation, environmental stewardship, and human ingenuity.

In the first section, "The Evolution of Cities," we delve into the historical roots of urbanization, tracing the fascinating journey from ancient settlements to the bustling metropolises of today. Understanding our past is essential to envisioning our future, for it provides us with insights into the core principles that make cities not just functional, but also enriching spaces for human life.

Moving forward, we explore the challenges faced by modern cities in "Challenges of Modern Cities." From overpopulation to environmental degradation, these challenges are daunting but not insurmountable. This section scrutinizes the obstacles that stand in the way of sustainable urban living, setting the stage for innovative solutions that will be explored in the chapters that follow.

The heart of our exploration lies in "Visionary Urban Concepts." This section is a testament to human imagination and ambition. Here, we encounter groundbreaking ideas that redefine the very fabric of urban living. Mixed-use megastructures, floating cities, and smart urban centers are just a glimpse of the innovative concepts that promise to shape our cities into eco-friendly, self-sustaining hubs of progress.

As we journey deeper, we unravel the intricate web of "Sustainable Urban Planning." From eco-friendly architecture to renewable energy solutions, this section dissects the essential components of sustainable cities. We explore the integration of technology into urban life, from smart grids to data-driven decision-making, painting a vivid picture of cities that respond dynamically to the needs of their inhabitants.

In "Green Spaces and Biodiversity," we step into the lush realms of nature within urban landscapes. Urban farming, green roofs, and biodiversity conservation efforts take center stage as we explore how cities can transform into environments that nurture both the human spirit and the natural world.

The chapters that follow dive into the core infrastructure of cities. "Urban Infrastructure Development" explores the importance of well-designed road networks, efficient traffic management, and the integration of technology to enhance urban mobility. "Clean Water Supply and Wastewater Management" examines the challenges of providing clean water to urban residents and delves into innovative methods for wastewater treatment and sustainable water management practices. In "Safe Living Spaces," we discuss the principles of safe housing design, earthquake-resistant structures, and fire safety measures, all of which contribute to creating secure environments for urban dwellers.

"Resilience and Climate Change Adaptation" scrutinizes innovative flood-resistant infrastructure, climate-responsive urban planning, and disaster preparedness initiatives. "Ethical Considerations in Future Cities" takes a closer look at privacy, environmental justice, and cultural inclusivity in urban policies, emphasizing the importance of ethical decision-making in shaping the cities of tomorrow.

The journey doesn't stop there. We peer into the future in "Future Trends and Speculations," exploring the possibilities of underwater cities, space-based habitats, and AI-driven urban management. The book culminates in a call to action, inviting readers to envision, plan, and create the future cities they want to inhabit.

Future Cities is more than a book; it's a manifesto for a sustainable urban revolution. It's an invitation to dream big, think green, and act now. Join us in this exploration of the cities that await us, where innovation, sustainability, and human flourishing converge to create a tomorrow that is not just bright but also green and vibrant.

Welcome to Future Cities.

Chapter 1: Introduction to Future Cities

Section 1.1: The Evolution of Cities

Cities have been the cradle of human civilization for centuries. In this section, we explore the fascinating journey of urban development. From ancient settlements to modern metropolises, we delve into the evolution of cities, tracing the historical and social factors that have shaped their growth. Understanding this evolution is crucial to grasp the challenges and opportunities faced by cities today.

Cities emerged as centers of trade, culture, and innovation in ancient civilizations. The concept of urban living transformed societies, giving rise to governance structures, diverse cultures, and economic activities. As populations grew, cities became hubs of knowledge, with scholars, artists, and thinkers congregating to exchange ideas.

The Industrial Revolution marked a significant turning point, leading to rapid urbanization and the rise of industrial cities. Factories, railways, and modern infrastructure transformed the urban landscape, drawing people from rural areas to seek employment and a better life. However, this growth also brought challenges such as overcrowding, pollution, and inadequate living conditions.

In the 20th century, cities continued to evolve, witnessing advancements in technology, transportation, and communication. The digital age further transformed cities into interconnected hubs, fostering globalization and cultural exchange. Today, cities stand at the forefront of innovation, with smart technologies shaping urban experiences.

In the pages that follow, we will explore key milestones in the evolution of cities and analyze the lessons learned from their history. Understanding our urban past is essential as we navigate the complexities of building sustainable and inclusive future cities.

Cities, the beating hearts of human civilization, have a rich and complex history that spans millennia. In this section, we embark on a captivating journey through time, tracing the evolution of cities from ancient settlements to the bustling metropolises of the modern era.

1.1.1 Early Urbanization: Seeds of Civilization

The story begins in ancient Mesopotamia, where the first cities emerged along the fertile banks of the Tigris and Euphrates rivers. These early urban centers were epicenters of agriculture, trade, and governance, laying the foundation for organized human societies. We explore the innovative irrigation techniques and architectural marvels of civilizations like Sumeria and Babylon, showcasing the remarkable ingenuity of our ancestors.

1.1.2 Classical Cities: Cradles of Knowledge

The ancient Greeks and Romans elevated city planning to an art form. Greek city-states like Athens fostered intellectual pursuits, giving birth to philosophy, democracy, and the concept of citizenship. Meanwhile, Rome's vast empire boasted magnificent cities adorned with aqueducts, forums, and amphitheaters. We delve into the architectural splendors of cities like Rome and Alexandria, examining how they became centers of knowledge and cultural exchange.

1.1.3 Medieval Marvels: From Castles to Cathedrals

The medieval period witnessed the rise of fortified cities, surrounded by walls and steeped in religious fervor. Magnificent cathedrals, such as Chartres in France and Cologne in Germany, became symbols of faith and architectural brilliance. We explore the evolution of medieval cities, examining the guild system, trade routes, and the birth of universities, highlighting how these urban centers became crucibles of art, science, and spirituality.

1.1.4 Renaissance and Enlightenment: Urban Revival

The Renaissance period ushered in a revival of classical ideals, leading to a resurgence in art, literature, and urban planning. Cities like Florence and Venice became patrons of the arts, nurturing talents like Leonardo da Vinci and Galileo Galilei. The Enlightenment further transformed cities, emphasizing reason, education, and democratic governance. We explore the intellectual salons of Paris, the coffeehouses of London, and the scientific academies of Amsterdam, showcasing how cities became catalysts for societal progress.

1.1.5 Industrial Revolution: Urbanization and Challenges

The 19th century witnessed unprecedented urbanization driven by the Industrial Revolution. Factories, railways, and steamships reshaped the urban landscape, drawing rural populations to industrial centers. Manchester, Birmingham, and Chicago became symbols of industrial prowess. However, this rapid growth also led to social inequalities, overcrowding, and unsanitary conditions. We delve into the challenges faced by these burgeoning cities, examining the efforts to improve public health, workers' rights, and urban infrastructure.

1.1.6 Modern Metropolises: Globalization and Innovation

The 20th and 21st centuries saw the rise of modern metropolises interconnected through global networks. New York, Tokyo, Shanghai, and Dubai stand as testaments to human ambition and architectural marvels. We explore the impact of globalization on cities, from the rise of skyscrapers to the integration of digital technologies. Themes such as multiculturalism, sustainability, and smart urban planning come to the fore as cities embrace innovation while addressing pressing challenges.

In the pages that follow, this section will offer a comprehensive exploration of the evolution of cities, providing readers with a nuanced understanding of the forces that have shaped urban landscapes throughout history.

Section 1.2: Challenges of Modern Cities

1.2.1 Overpopulation: Striving for Sustainable Urban Growth

Rapid urbanization and population influx strain city resources, leading to challenges like housing shortages and overcrowded public services. Urban planners grapple with fostering sustainable growth by implementing innovative housing solutions such as eco-friendly high-rises, mixed-use developments, and smart city planning. These strategies not only accommodate the growing population but also ensure a harmonious balance with the urban environment.

1.2.2 Pollution and Environmental Degradation: The Imperative of Green Urbanism

Urban areas grapple with pollution from various sources, affecting both the environment and public health. Cities are addressing these challenges through the widespread adoption of green urbanism. Initiatives include the integration of renewable energy sources, the implementation of zero-emission public transportation, and the creation of urban green spaces. Additionally, stringent environmental regulations and sustainable waste management practices are pivotal in mitigating pollution and preserving the city's natural ecosystem.

1.2.3 Strain on Urban Infrastructure: Innovations for Resilient Cities

Urban infrastructure faces increasing demands due to population growth and technological advancements. To alleviate this strain, cities are embracing cutting-edge technologies such as smart grids, IoT-enabled utilities, and 3D-printed infrastructure components. Furthermore, investing in resilient designs, such as earthquake-resistant buildings and flood-proof infrastructure, ensures cities can withstand natural disasters and rapidly recover, minimizing disruptions to residents' lives.

1.2.4 Social Disparities: Empowering Communities for Inclusive Growth

Social disparities persist in urban areas, hindering progress and social cohesion. Cities are fostering inclusive growth through targeted educational programs, vocational training centers, and affordable healthcare clinics in underserved communities. Entrepreneurship initiatives, micro-financing opportunities, and cultural exchange events empower marginalized populations, fostering a sense of belonging and active participation in the city's economic and social fabric.

In the upcoming pages, we will delve even deeper, examining case studies from diverse cities around the globe. By understanding the unique challenges faced by each city and the tailored solutions they implement, we gain valuable insights into the diverse strategies that can be employed to create resilient, sustainable, and inclusive future cities.

Section 1.3: Visionary Urban Concepts

1.3.1 Vertical Forests and Sky Gardens: A Green Revolution in the Sky

Vertical forests, characterized by skyscrapers covered in lush greenery, and sky gardens suspended amid high-rises, represent a paradigm shift in urban architecture. These innovative designs transform concrete jungles into oxygen-rich ecosystems. Vertical forests not only enhance urban aesthetics but also contribute to carbon sequestration, air purification, and biodiversity conservation. Sky gardens, offering serene spaces amidst the urban hustle, exemplify the fusion of nature and modern living, revolutionizing the concept of green spaces in cities.

Vertical forests and sky gardens represent a paradigm shift in urban design, introducing a harmonious coexistence between nature and architecture. In this section, we explore the intricate details of these revolutionary concepts, examining their ecological impact, architectural innovations, and the transformative effect they have on urban living.

1.3.1.1 Ecological Significance: Creating Urban Biodiversity Hotspots

Vertical forests serve as green lungs within the heart of urban landscapes. These towering structures, adorned with a rich tapestry of flora, contribute significantly to urban biodiversity. The diverse plant species attract birds, insects, and other wildlife, transforming these buildings into thriving ecosystems. Sky gardens, strategically placed at various levels of skyscrapers, serve as pollinator hubs, enhancing the local flora and supporting the essential ecosystem services provided by bees and butterflies.

1.3.1.2 Air Quality and Carbon Sequestration: Nature's Contribution to Urban Health

One of the most significant benefits of vertical forests and sky gardens is their role in improving air quality. Through photosynthesis, plants absorb carbon dioxide and release oxygen, purifying the air in densely populated urban areas. These green structures act as natural air filters, trapping pollutants and particulate matter, thus mitigating the adverse health effects associated with poor air quality. Additionally, the collective biomass of these structures aids in carbon sequestration, making them vital contributors to the fight against climate change.

1.3.1.3 Architectural Innovations: Designing for Sustainability and Aesthetics

Architects and engineers are pioneering innovative techniques to incorporate greenery seamlessly into skyscraper designs. Specialized planting systems, hydroponic technology, and lightweight soil compositions are employed to ensure the health and stability of the vegetation. Additionally, architects focus on creating aesthetically pleasing designs, where the greenery complements the building's architecture, enhancing the overall visual appeal of the cityscape. These innovative approaches redefine the relationship between nature and urban infrastructure, setting new standards for sustainable architectural practices.

1.3.1.4 Community Engagement and Well-Being: Fostering Social Cohesion

Vertical forests and sky gardens not only benefit the environment but also enhance the well-being of urban residents. These green spaces provide sanctuaries for relaxation and recreation, offering residents a respite from the fast-paced urban life. Community engagement programs, such as gardening workshops and environmental awareness events, empower residents to actively participate in the maintenance and cultivation of these green spaces. The sense of ownership fosters social cohesion, strengthening the community fabric and creating a shared commitment to environmental stewardship.

1.3.1.5 Economic Viability and Urban Renewal: Green Investments for the Future

Investing in vertical forests and sky gardens offers significant economic advantages. These green structures increase property values, making them attractive investments for developers. Additionally, they stimulate economic activities in surrounding areas, fostering a vibrant local economy. Furthermore, urban renewal projects centered around green architecture rejuvenate neglected urban spaces, transforming them into thriving hubs of activity. The economic viability of these projects positions them as essential components of sustainable urban development, encouraging further investments in green infrastructure.

In the pages that follow, we will continue our exploration of visionary urban concepts, delving into the intricacies of mixed-use megastructures, floating cities, underwater habitats, and smart cities. Each concept represents a revolutionary approach to urban living, promising a future where cities seamlessly integrate with the natural world while fostering innovation, sustainability, and community well-being.

1.3.2 Mixed-Use Megastructures: Communities in Vertical Cities

Mixed-use megastructures redefine urban living by integrating residential, commercial, and recreational spaces within colossal complexes. This visionary approach aims to optimize land use, minimize commuting, and foster vibrant communities. Vertical integration of various functions within these megastructures promotes social interaction, creates self-sustained microcosms, and reduces the ecological footprint. By challenging traditional city layouts, these megastructures represent a leap towards sustainable, cohesive urban living.

In the pursuit of sustainable urban living, mixed-use megastructures have emerged as transformative marvels, reshaping the very essence of cities. This section delves deep into the intricacies of these colossal complexes, where residential, commercial, and recreational spaces intertwine, giving rise to self-contained urban microcosms that challenge traditional city layouts and elevate the quality of urban life.

1.3.2.1 Optimizing Land Use: Vertical Integration as a Solution

One of the key objectives of mixed-use megastructures is the efficient utilization of limited urban space. By vertically integrating various functions, these structures optimize land use, allowing cities to accommodate growing populations without sprawling horizontally. Residential apartments coexist with office spaces, shopping centers, and entertainment venues, all within the same towering edifice. This vertical integration not only conserves valuable land but also fosters a dynamic synergy between different aspects of urban living.

1.3.2.2 Minimizing Commuting: A Vision for Urban Connectivity

The integration of residential and workplace areas within mixed-use megastructures minimizes the need for extensive commuting. Residents find themselves mere elevators away from their workplaces, reducing traffic congestion and diminishing the environmental impact associated with daily commuting. The proximity of commercial spaces ensures convenience, while the availability of recreational amenities within the same structure promotes a healthy work-life balance. This radical reduction in commuting time enhances productivity and enriches the overall urban experience.

1.3.2.3 Fostering Vibrant Communities: Social Interaction at Every Level

Mixed-use megastructures foster vibrant communities by encouraging social interaction at every level. Shared spaces, such as communal gardens, rooftop parks, and co-working areas, create opportunities for residents, workers, and visitors to connect and collaborate. The seamless blend of living, working, and recreational spaces nurtures a sense of community, breaking down the barriers often associated with traditional urban layouts. Cultural events, art installations, and communal activities further enhance social cohesion, transforming these megastructures into thriving hubs of human interaction and creativity.

1.3.2.4 Creating Self-Sustained Microcosms: Urban Ecosystems within Walls

These megastructures are designed as self-sustained microcosms, incorporating features such as rainwater harvesting, solar energy generation, and waste recycling systems. Green spaces within the structure enhance air quality and provide recreational areas for residents. Innovative technologies, including vertical farming and aquaponics, promote sustainable food production within the complex. These self-sustained ecosystems not only reduce the strain on external resources but also serve as models for eco-friendly urban living, showcasing the potential for cities to become self-sufficient in essential resources.

1.3.2.5 Reducing the Ecological Footprint: A Leap towards Sustainability

By challenging traditional city layouts and promoting compact urban living, mixed-use megastructures significantly reduce the ecological footprint of cities. The vertical integration of functions minimizes the need for expansive infrastructure and transportation networks, conserving energy and resources. Additionally, the incorporation of green technologies, energy-efficient design, and waste management practices further diminishes the environmental impact. These structures exemplify the future of sustainable, cohesive urban living, setting a precedent for environmentally conscious urban development worldwide.

In the upcoming pages, we will continue our exploration, delving into the innovative concepts of floating cities, underwater habitats, and smart cities. Each concept represents a bold step towards a future where urban environments seamlessly blend with nature, fostering innovation, sustainability, and community well-being.

1.3.3 Floating Cities and Underwater Habitats: Cities Adrift and Submerged

Floating cities, designed to float on water bodies, and underwater habitats, nestled beneath the ocean's surface, present innovative solutions to the challenges posed by rising sea levels. These concepts explore advanced engineering, sustainable energy sources, and closed-loop waste management systems. Floating cities incorporate renewable energy platforms, desalination facilities, and aquaponic farms, ensuring self-sufficiency. Underwater habitats leverage marine resources while prioritizing ecological balance. These concepts offer a glimpse into humanity's potential to adapt to changing environments, paving the way for resilient coastal communities.

In the face of rising sea levels, humanity has turned to the vast expanse of water bodies as a canvas for innovative urban solutions. Floating cities, designed to gracefully float on the water's surface, and underwater habitats, nestled beneath the ocean's embrace, represent bold ventures into the future of coastal living. This section immerses us in the intricacies of these concepts, unveiling the advanced engineering, sustainable energy sources, and closed-loop waste management systems that make them not just viable but pioneering examples of resilient urban design.

1.3.3.1 Advanced Engineering: Floating on the Horizon

Floating cities are marvels of engineering, designed to withstand the ebb and flow of the tides and the challenges posed by changing weather patterns. These cities employ state-of-the-art materials, including lightweight yet durable composites, to create floating platforms that ensure stability and safety. Innovative anchoring systems and dynamic mooring technologies enable these cities to navigate coastal waters while remaining securely tethered, showcasing human ingenuity in adapting to maritime environments.

1.3.3.2 Sustainable Energy Sources: Harnessing Nature's Power

The energy demands of floating cities are met through renewable sources that harness the power of nature. Solar panels adorn the cityscape, soaking in the sun's energy and providing electricity for lighting, heating, and appliances. Wind turbines, strategically positioned to capture the ocean breezes, generate additional clean energy. These sustainable energy sources not only power the city but also serve as a testament to the harmonious integration of human habitats with the natural elements, fostering a symbiotic relationship with the environment.

1.3.3.3 Closed-Loop Waste Management: Recycling Resources at Sea

Floating cities are pioneers in closed-loop waste management systems, where every resource is carefully recycled and repurposed. Advanced water filtration and desalination facilities ensure a constant supply of clean, potable water. Waste, including organic matter, is processed through innovative composting methods and aquaponic farms. These closed-loop systems minimize waste discharge into the ocean, preserving the marine ecosystem and creating a sustainable, circular approach to resource management in the maritime environment.

1.3.3.4 Underwater Habitats: Nurturing Ecological Balance

Beneath the ocean's surface, underwater habitats explore the delicate balance between human habitation and marine ecosystems. These habitats are designed to minimize environmental impact, using non-intrusive construction methods that preserve coral reefs and marine biodiversity. Aquaculture initiatives within these habitats promote sustainable fish farming, reducing the pressure on wild fish populations. Additionally, careful waste management systems prevent pollution, ensuring that the delicate underwater ecosystems remain intact and thrive alongside human inhabitants.

1.3.3.5 Human Adaptation: Pioneering Resilient Coastal Communities

Floating cities and underwater habitats represent the pinnacle of human adaptation to changing environments. These innovative concepts challenge traditional notions of urban living, offering a glimpse into the future of resilient coastal communities. By embracing the vastness of the oceans and harnessing the power of sustainable technologies, humanity pioneers a new era where cities gracefully float on water bodies and coexist harmoniously with the depths of the ocean, setting the stage for a future where coastal living is synonymous with sustainability and resilience.

In the upcoming pages, our exploration will extend to the realm of smart cities, where the fusion of technology and urban living promises to revolutionize the way we inhabit and interact with our environments, further shaping the cities of tomorrow.

1.3.4 Smart Cities and IoT Integration:
Where Technology Shapes Urban Life

Smart cities harness the power of the Internet of Things (IoT) to enhance urban efficiency, sustainability, and resident well-being. IoT-enabled sensors and data analytics optimize traffic flow, energy consumption, and waste management. Citizen engagement platforms promote participatory governance, empowering residents to actively shape their urban environment. From intelligent transportation systems to real-time environmental monitoring, smart cities exemplify the harmonious integration of technology into the urban fabric, promising a future where cities respond dynamically to the needs of their inhabitants.

In the digital age, the convergence of technology and urban living has given rise to smart cities, where the Internet of Things (IoT) plays a pivotal role in revolutionizing urban landscapes. This section immerses us in the world of smart cities, exploring the intricate web of IoT-enabled sensors, data analytics, and citizen engagement platforms that enhance urban efficiency, sustainability, and the well-being of residents. From optimizing traffic flow to promoting participatory governance, smart cities exemplify the harmonious integration of technology into the very fabric of urban life, promising a future where cities respond dynamically to the needs and aspirations of their inhabitants.

1.3.4.1 IoT-Enabled Sensors: The Nervous System of Smart Cities

At the heart of smart cities lies a network of IoT-enabled sensors, strategically placed throughout the urban landscape. These sensors act as the city's nervous system, collecting real-time data on various parameters such as traffic flow, air quality, and energy consumption. Equipped with advanced sensing technologies, these devices provide a continuous stream of data that serves as the foundation for informed decision-making, allowing cities to respond promptly to emerging challenges and optimize resource allocation.

1.3.4.2 Data Analytics: Transforming Raw Data into Actionable Insights

The vast amount of data collected by IoT sensors is transformed into actionable insights through sophisticated data analytics. Machine learning algorithms and artificial intelligence processes analyze the data, identifying patterns, trends, and anomalies. These insights empower urban planners and policymakers to make data-driven decisions, enhancing efficiency in areas such as traffic management, waste collection, and energy distribution. By leveraging data analytics, smart cities optimize their operations, reduce costs, and improve overall urban quality of life.

1.3.4.3 Optimizing Traffic Flow: Intelligent Transportation Systems

Smart cities revolutionize urban mobility through Intelligent Transportation Systems (ITS). IoT-enabled traffic sensors and real-time data analysis facilitate dynamic traffic management, optimizing signal timings, and rerouting vehicles to alleviate congestion. Smart traffic lights adapt in real-time to traffic volumes, reducing wait times and enhancing the flow of vehicles. Additionally, IoT-connected public transportation systems provide commuters with real-time schedules and updates, encouraging the use of eco-friendly modes of transport and reducing the city's carbon footprint.

1.3.4.4 Citizen Engagement Platforms: Empowering Urban Residents

Citizen engagement platforms bridge the gap between residents and urban governance, fostering participatory governance in smart cities. Mobile applications and online platforms enable residents to report issues, provide feedback, and participate in community initiatives. These platforms promote transparency, accountability, and active citizen involvement in shaping the urban environment. Citizens become co-creators of their cities, actively contributing to the decision-making process and ensuring that urban development aligns with the needs and desires of the community.

1.3.4.5 Real-time Environmental Monitoring: Preserving Urban Ecosystems

Environmental sustainability is a cornerstone of smart cities, facilitated by real-time monitoring of urban ecosystems. IoT sensors continuously assess air and water quality, noise levels, and green spaces. Immediate alerts regarding pollution spikes or environmental hazards enable rapid response measures, safeguarding the well-being of residents and the natural environment. Smart irrigation systems, guided by real-time weather data, optimize water usage in public parks and gardens, conserving this precious resource and promoting a sustainable urban ecology.

In the upcoming pages, our exploration will continue to unfold, delving deeper into various aspects of future cities, examining innovative approaches, and visionary concepts that collectively shape the cities of tomorrow.

Chapter 2: Urban Infrastructure Development

Urban areas rely heavily on well-designed and safe road networks, serving as the lifelines of bustling cities. This chapter delves into the critical aspects of road infrastructure, emphasizing the significance of safe roads in the development of future cities.

Section 2.1: Road Infrastructure and Safety Measures

Importance of Well-Designed Roads:

Well-designed roads are the backbone of urban mobility. They ensure smooth traffic flow, reduce congestion, and enhance the overall accessibility of a city. Properly planned road networks accommodate the diverse needs of pedestrians, cyclists, and motorists, fostering a sense of connectivity and ease of travel. Urban planners prioritize the integration of sidewalks, bike lanes, and dedicated lanes for public transport to create a holistic and inclusive road system.

Strategies for Road Safety:

Ensuring road safety is paramount to the well-being of urban dwellers. This section explores comprehensive strategies aimed at minimizing accidents and enhancing pedestrian safety.

Initiatives such as traffic calming measures, improved street lighting, and clear signage contribute to creating safer road environments. Public awareness campaigns educate both drivers and pedestrians, emphasizing the importance of mutual respect and adherence to traffic rules, fostering a culture of safety and responsibility.

Efficient Traffic Management:

Efficient traffic management is essential for preventing gridlock and optimizing the flow of vehicles. Innovative solutions, including intelligent traffic signal systems, predictive traffic modeling, and real-time data analysis, play a crucial role in managing traffic patterns. By leveraging advanced technologies, cities can mitigate congestion and enhance the overall commuting experience for residents. Additionally, dynamic traffic management systems adapt to real-time conditions, rerouting traffic to less congested routes and minimizing travel time.

Integration of Technology to Enhance Road Infrastructure:

The integration of technology revolutionizes urban roadways. This section investigates the role of smart technologies, such as sensors, IoT devices, and data analytics, in enhancing road infrastructure. Smart roads can adapt to traffic patterns in real-time, optimize traffic signals based on demand, and provide valuable data for urban planners to make informed decisions about infrastructure improvements. Furthermore, augmented reality interfaces can provide real-time information to drivers, alerting them to potential hazards, diversions, and weather conditions, ensuring a safer and more informed commute.

Sustainable Road Development:

Sustainability is key in modern urban planning. Explore eco-friendly road construction materials, solar-powered streetlights, and permeable pavements that allow rainwater to replenish the ground, reducing the strain on drainage systems. Sustainable road development not only minimizes the environmental impact but also contributes to the overall resilience of the city. Green roads, adorned with trees and vegetation, act as natural carbon sinks, improving air quality and enhancing the urban environment. Moreover, sustainable roadways integrate charging infrastructure for electric vehicles, promoting the adoption of clean transportation alternatives and reducing greenhouse gas emissions.

In the subsequent sections, our exploration will extend to other crucial aspects of urban infrastructure, including water supply systems, wastewater management, and the integration of green spaces within cities. Each component is integral to the holistic development of future cities, creating environments that are not only functional but also sustainable and safe for all residents.

Section 2.2: Clean Water Supply and Wastewater Management

The availability of clean and accessible water is a fundamental necessity for any urban area. However, ensuring a sustainable supply of clean water to meet the demands of a growing urban population presents numerous challenges. This section explores the complexities of providing clean water to urban residents and delves into innovative methods for wastewater treatment, water recycling, and sustainable water management practices.

Challenges in Providing Clean and Accessible Water:

Urban centers face multifaceted challenges in supplying clean and accessible water. Rapid urbanization, aging infrastructure, and pollution are significant hurdles. Ensuring a consistent supply of potable water to every household while maintaining water quality standards demands meticulous planning. Additionally, the equitable distribution of water resources across diverse socioeconomic areas necessitates careful consideration, promoting social inclusion and addressing disparities.

Innovative Wastewater Treatment Methods:

Effective wastewater treatment is vital to preserving water quality and environmental health. This section explores advanced wastewater treatment methods such as biological treatment processes, membrane bioreactors, and chemical disinfection techniques. Innovative approaches like constructed wetlands and decentralized wastewater treatment systems are examined for their efficiency in purifying wastewater before it re-enters natural water bodies. Moreover, the integration of natural filtration processes and biofiltration systems helps in removing contaminants, ensuring that treated water is environmentally friendly and safe for reuse.

Water Recycling and Reuse:

Water recycling and reuse are pivotal in sustainable urban water management. This segment investigates water recycling methods such as greywater systems, where lightly used water from sinks and showers is treated and repurposed for non-potable applications like irrigation and toilet flushing. Additionally, blackwater treatment systems, capable of purifying wastewater from toilets, are explored. These innovative systems, when combined with rigorous water quality monitoring, facilitate the safe reuse of water resources, conserving freshwater supplies and reducing the overall strain on urban water networks.

Sustainable Water Management Practices:

Sustainable water management practices are essential for the long-term viability of urban areas. This part of the section delves into rainwater harvesting systems, capturing and storing rainwater for various uses, including irrigation and groundwater recharge. The implementation of smart water grids equipped with sensors and real-time monitoring tools optimizes water distribution, minimizes leakages, and enhances overall efficiency. Furthermore, community engagement initiatives promote water conservation awareness, encouraging residents to adopt water-saving habits, thereby ensuring the sustainable use of this precious resource.

In the subsequent sections, our exploration will extend to other critical aspects of urban infrastructure, including energy distribution networks, waste-to-energy solutions, and the integration of smart technologies within cities. Each component contributes to the creation of resilient and sustainable urban environments, fostering a high quality of life for residents while safeguarding natural resources for future generations.

Section 2.3: Advanced Wastewater Filtering Technologies

Wastewater management stands as a critical component of urban infrastructure, demanding advanced technologies to ensure the safe disposal and recycling of water. This section delves into the forefront of wastewater filtration and purification technologies, exploring methods that are reshaping urban sanitation systems, enhancing efficiency, and promoting environmental sustainability.

Membrane Bioreactors (MBRs):

Membrane bioreactors represent a significant advancement in wastewater treatment. In this innovative technology, a combination of biological treatment and membrane filtration is employed. Microorganisms break down organic pollutants in the wastewater, and the membranes act as a barrier, allowing only purified water molecules to pass through. MBRs provide a compact and highly efficient solution, producing high-quality treated water that meets stringent quality standards. Their flexibility in handling varying wastewater compositions makes them invaluable in urban environments with diverse industrial discharges.

UV Disinfection:

Ultraviolet (UV) disinfection is a cutting-edge method employed after primary treatment processes to kill harmful microorganisms in wastewater. UV light disrupts the DNA of bacteria, viruses, and other pathogens, rendering them inactive. Unlike traditional chemical disinfection, UV disinfection leaves no residual chemicals in the treated water, making it an eco-friendly and safe alternative. Urban areas benefit from UV disinfection systems, ensuring that the water released back into natural water bodies is free from harmful microbes, safeguarding both aquatic life and public health.

Advanced Chemical Treatments:

Advancements in chemical treatments have led to the development of novel substances capable of efficiently precipitating and removing contaminants from wastewater. These chemicals react with pollutants, forming larger particles that can be easily separated from the water. Additionally, coagulants and flocculants, when used judiciously, enhance the settling of suspended solids. Advanced chemical treatments are tailored to specific pollutants, ensuring targeted removal and promoting the reuse of treated water for non-potable purposes, such as irrigation and industrial processes.

Integration of Smart Sensors and Monitoring:

The integration of smart sensors and real-time monitoring systems revolutionizes wastewater treatment. These sensors continuously analyze water quality parameters, allowing for immediate adjustments in the treatment process based on real-time data. Smart monitoring ensures the optimal performance of treatment plants, enhances energy efficiency, and minimizes chemical usage. Moreover, predictive analytics based on historical data enable proactive maintenance, reducing downtime and ensuring uninterrupted wastewater treatment operations in urban areas.

In conclusion, the deployment of these advanced wastewater filtering technologies marks a pivotal step toward sustainable urban development. By investing in cutting-edge methods such as membrane bioreactors, UV disinfection, advanced chemical treatments, and smart sensor integration, cities can uphold environmental standards, conserve water resources, and protect public health. As we move forward, the exploration will extend to other critical aspects of urban infrastructure, shaping cities that are not only efficient and resilient but also environmentally responsible and technologically advanced.

Chapter 3: Safe Living Spaces

Section 3.1: Safe Housing Design and Construction

Ensuring the safety and well-being of urban residents begins with the fundamental aspect of their living spaces. This section delves deep into the principles of safe housing design and construction, exploring innovative approaches and architectural techniques that prioritize the resilience of structures, the safety of inhabitants, and the environmental sustainability of urban dwellings.

Earthquake-Resistant Structures:

In earthquake-prone regions, constructing buildings that can withstand seismic forces is paramount. Engineers employ a variety of techniques such as base isolation, damping systems, and flexible materials to absorb and dissipate seismic energy. Additionally, innovative foundation designs distribute the earthquake forces evenly, preventing structural damage. By integrating these earthquake-resistant features, urban areas mitigate the risks associated with seismic activities, ensuring the safety of residents even in the face of natural disasters.

Fire Safety Measures:

Fire safety is a critical aspect of housing design, particularly in densely populated urban environments. Advanced fire-resistant materials, automated sprinkler systems, smoke detectors, and fire-resistant compartmentalization within buildings are essential components of modern housing design. Evacuation plans, clearly marked exit routes, and fire-resistant building codes further enhance the safety of residents. By implementing these measures, cities reduce the risk of fire-related disasters, safeguarding lives and property.

Eco-Friendly Materials and Sustainable Construction:

The choice of construction materials significantly impacts both the environment and the inhabitants' health. Utilizing eco-friendly materials, such as reclaimed wood, recycled steel, and low-emission adhesives, reduces the carbon footprint of buildings. Sustainable construction practices, like passive solar design and natural ventilation, minimize energy consumption and promote environmentally responsible living. Furthermore, integrating green roofs and rainwater harvesting systems not only enhances energy efficiency but also contributes to urban biodiversity and water conservation efforts.

Innovative Architectural Approaches:

Innovative architects are exploring new paradigms that redefine housing design. Concepts like modular construction, where building components are prefabricated in controlled environments and assembled on-site, streamline construction processes and reduce waste. Additionally, the incorporation of biophilic design principles, connecting residents with nature through elements like indoor gardens and natural light, enhances well-being and mental health. Smart home technologies further improve residents' quality of life, providing energy efficiency, security, and convenience.

In conclusion, safe housing design and construction represent the cornerstone of urban resilience and the well-being of its inhabitants. By embracing earthquake-resistant structures, robust fire safety measures, eco-friendly materials, and innovative architectural approaches, cities create living spaces that not only withstand environmental challenges but also foster healthier, happier communities. As we move forward, the exploration will extend to other vital aspects of urban safety and community well-being, ensuring cities that are not just secure, but also sustainable and supportive of the flourishing lives of their residents.

Section 3.2: Earthquake-Resistant Buildings and Infrastructure

Urban areas located in seismic zones face significant challenges in ensuring the safety of their inhabitants and preserving critical infrastructure during earthquakes. This section delves into the realm of earthquake-resistant construction, exploring advanced engineering techniques, innovative materials, and stringent building codes aimed at minimizing seismic vulnerabilities in urban environments.

Advanced Engineering Techniques:

Engineers employ cutting-edge techniques to design buildings capable of withstanding seismic forces. One such approach is base isolation, where structures are placed on flexible bearings that absorb seismic energy. Additionally, damping systems, such as tuned mass dampers and viscous dampers, dissipate vibrations, enhancing stability during earthquakes. Reinforced concrete frames and shear walls provide structural integrity, distributing seismic forces uniformly throughout the building. By integrating these techniques, urban areas create a robust foundation for earthquake-resistant construction, ensuring structures remain standing and occupants safe even during intense seismic events.

Seismic Retrofitting:

Retrofitting existing buildings is a crucial aspect of earthquake resilience. Engineers utilize various methods like adding steel braces, reinforcing walls, and upgrading foundations to enhance the seismic performance of older structures. Strengthening the building's skeleton, particularly in vulnerable areas, ensures that the entire structure can withstand seismic shaking. Additionally, retrofitting critical infrastructure such as bridges and dams is essential to maintaining vital lifelines in the aftermath of an earthquake. Urban areas invest in comprehensive retrofitting programs, preserving historic landmarks and modern structures alike, while safeguarding lives and minimizing economic losses.

Foundation Design and Soil Analysis:

Understanding the geological and geotechnical aspects of the land is fundamental in earthquake-resistant construction. Engineers conduct thorough soil analysis to determine the site's seismic vulnerability. Special foundation designs, such as deep foundations and pile foundations, are employed in areas with soft or liquefiable soils, ensuring stability during earthquakes. By adapting foundation designs to the unique characteristics of the land, urban areas mitigate the risks associated with ground shaking, creating a resilient foundation for buildings and infrastructure.

Stringent Building Codes and Regulations:

Stringent building codes and regulations are the backbone of earthquake-resistant construction. Cities enforce codes that dictate the use of specific materials, design parameters, and construction techniques aimed at enhancing seismic resilience. These codes evolve with advancements in engineering knowledge, ensuring that new constructions are at the forefront of seismic safety. Regular inspections and rigorous adherence to these codes are essential, guaranteeing that urban areas are well-prepared to face seismic challenges, thereby safeguarding the lives and livelihoods of their residents.

In conclusion, earthquake-resistant buildings and infrastructure are vital components of urban resilience. By incorporating advanced engineering techniques, implementing seismic retrofitting measures, understanding foundation design principles, and enforcing stringent building codes, cities in seismic zones create environments that can withstand the forces of nature. This not only preserves lives and property but also fosters a sense of security and stability among urban inhabitants, ensuring that cities can swiftly recover and thrive in the face of seismic adversity. As our exploration continues, we will delve into additional aspects of disaster preparedness and community resilience, painting a comprehensive portrait of urban areas that are not only prepared for disasters but also capable of thriving in their aftermath.

Section 3.3: Business Buildings and Apartments: Ensuring Structural Integrity

Explore the challenges and solutions related to constructing safe business buildings and apartments. Discuss the role of architects, engineers, and urban planners in ensuring the structural integrity and safety of commercial and residential complexes.

Constructing safe business buildings and apartments is paramount for urban areas, ensuring the well-being of residents and the functionality of commercial spaces. This section explores the intricate challenges faced in the construction of these structures and delves into the collaborative efforts of architects, engineers, and urban planners in guaranteeing their structural integrity and safety.

Architectural Innovation and Safety:

Architects play a pivotal role in designing business buildings and apartments that are both aesthetically pleasing and structurally sound. They integrate innovative architectural approaches, such as open floor plans and flexible spaces, while ensuring adherence to safety standards. Collaborative design processes involve thorough risk assessments, identifying potential vulnerabilities and devising architectural solutions that enhance the buildings' resistance to seismic forces and other hazards.

Engineering Expertise in Structural Design:

Structural engineers are instrumental in ensuring the robustness of business buildings and apartments. They employ advanced engineering principles to calculate loads, stresses, and potential points of failure. By employing materials with high tensile strength and employing cutting-edge construction techniques, engineers create structures capable of withstanding various stressors, including earthquakes and extreme weather events. Moreover, they oversee the incorporation of seismic bracing, reinforced concrete cores, and other essential elements that enhance the structural stability of high-rise buildings, guaranteeing the safety of occupants.

Urban Planning for Community Safety:

Urban planners work hand-in-hand with architects and engineers to integrate business buildings and apartments seamlessly into the urban fabric. They focus on the spatial arrangement of structures, ensuring safe distances between buildings to prevent potential domino effects during disasters. Additionally, they strategize evacuation routes, emergency access points, and green spaces that enhance overall safety. Collaborative urban planning endeavors prioritize mixed-use zoning, fostering vibrant communities where residential spaces, offices, and recreational areas coexist harmoniously, enhancing the overall quality of urban life.

Stringent Building Codes and Regulations:

Adherence to stringent building codes and regulations is non-negotiable in ensuring the safety of business buildings and apartments. Cities enforce codes that dictate the use of fire-resistant materials, emergency exits, and fire suppression systems, minimizing the risks associated with fire emergencies. Regular inspections and certifications validate the structures' compliance, offering reassurance to residents and business owners alike.

In conclusion, the construction of safe business buildings and apartments is a multifaceted process that demands meticulous planning, innovative design, and rigorous adherence to safety protocols. The collaborative efforts of architects, engineers, and urban planners, coupled with stringent building codes, create urban spaces that prioritize the well-being of inhabitants. These efforts not only guarantee structural integrity but also foster thriving, secure communities. As our exploration continues, we will delve further into the intricacies of safe living spaces, addressing additional aspects of architectural innovation, disaster preparedness, and community resilience.

Chapter 4: Sustainable Urban Planning

Section 4.1: Eco-Friendly Architecture:

Building for a Greener Future

As the world grapples with environmental challenges, architects and urban planners are pioneering eco-friendly architecture, ushering in a new era of sustainable construction practices. In this section, we delve into innovative building materials, green roofs, and passive design techniques that minimize the ecological impact of construction projects. From reclaimed materials to energy-efficient designs, architects are redefining the blueprint of urban structures, showcasing how sustainable architecture can harmonize with the natural environment.

4.1.1 Reclaimed and Recycled Materials:

Building with a Purpose

Eco-friendly architecture emphasizes the use of reclaimed and recycled materials, transforming discarded items into essential building components. From recycled steel and reclaimed wood to repurposed glass and plastic, architects are harnessing the potential of discarded materials, reducing waste and conserving resources. Through creative engineering, these materials find new life in construction, demonstrating how sustainability can be at the core of architectural innovation.

In the realm of eco-friendly architecture, the ethos of sustainability extends far beyond design—it permeates the very materials used in construction. Architects and builders are embracing the concept of circularity, where discarded materials are reincarnated into vital building components. This section immerses us in the world of reclaimed and recycled materials, unveiling the creative engineering that breathes new life into discarded items, demonstrating how sustainability forms the bedrock of architectural innovation.

4.1.1.1 Recycled Steel: The Backbone of Green Structures

Recycled steel, salvaged from decommissioned structures or industrial waste, serves as the backbone of eco-friendly buildings. Through advanced smelting and purification processes, discarded steel is transformed into beams, pillars, and frameworks. These recycled steel components not only retain the structural integrity of their virgin counterparts but also significantly reduce the demand for raw steel production. By repurposing steel, architects contribute to the conservation of natural resources and minimize the carbon footprint associated with steel manufacturing.

4.1.1.2 Reclaimed Wood: Preserving History in Modern Architecture

Reclaimed wood tells a story of its own, bearing the marks of time and history. Salvaged from old barns, warehouses, or decommissioned ships, reclaimed wood finds new purpose in contemporary architecture. Architects craft elegant flooring, sturdy beams, and decorative accents from this weathered timber, adding a touch of rustic charm to modern designs. By incorporating reclaimed wood, architects not only preserve the heritage of the past but also alleviate the pressure on living forests, promoting sustainable forestry practices and biodiversity conservation.

4.1.1.3 Repurposed Glass: From Discards to Dazzling Facades

Discarded glass, once destined for landfills, undergoes a remarkable transformation in the hands of innovative architects. Through recycling processes, old glass bottles and windows are pulverized and reformed into sleek, energy-efficient panels. These repurposed glass panels adorn building facades, allowing natural light to permeate interiors while providing insulation. Glass curtain walls made from recycled materials not only reduce the energy demands of buildings but also showcase the aesthetic potential of sustainable design, turning overlooked waste into architectural elegance.

4.1.1.4 Reimagined Plastic: From Pollution to Practicality

Plastic waste, a global environmental concern, finds new life in the hands of eco-conscious architects. Through meticulous sorting and processing, discarded plastic is transformed into durable construction materials. Recycled plastic composites serve as alternatives to traditional materials in decking, flooring, and even structural elements. By reimagining plastic waste, architects mitigate plastic pollution, contribute to the circular economy, and pioneer innovative solutions that repurpose a material once considered disposable into indispensable components of sustainable architecture.

In the upcoming sections, our exploration will extend to green roofs, passive design techniques, and net-zero energy buildings, unraveling a comprehensive vision of sustainable urban planning and design. Each element we explore represents a crucial building block in the creation of cities that not only endure but thrive, harmonizing with the environment and fostering resilient, vibrant communities.

4.1.2 Green Roofs and Living Walls:

Nature in the Urban Skyline

Green roofs and living walls represent a fusion of nature and urban infrastructure. Green roofs, adorned with vegetation, provide insulation, absorb rainwater, and offer habitats for birds and insects. Living walls, vertical gardens covering building facades, enhance aesthetics and air quality. Together, these features transform concrete jungles into vibrant ecosystems, introducing biodiversity to the urban landscape and mitigating the heat island effect. Architects are integrating these elements into their designs, creating visually stunning and ecologically beneficial urban environments.

In the bustling landscapes of urban centers, a transformative fusion of nature and architecture is taking place, reshaping the very essence of cities. Green roofs, adorned with lush vegetation, and living walls, vertical gardens that grace building facades, are at the forefront of this green revolution. This section immerses us in the beauty and functionality of these living elements, unraveling the ecological benefits they bring to urban environments. From enhancing aesthetics to improving air quality, green roofs and living walls redefine the urban skyline, transforming concrete jungles into thriving ecosystems and mitigating the heat island effect.

4.1.2.1 Green Roofs: Insulation, Rainwater Absorption, and Biodiversity

Green roofs are veritable oases atop urban buildings. Covered in a variety of plant species, these roofs provide natural insulation, reducing energy consumption for both heating and cooling. Moreover, they serve as sponges, absorbing rainwater and mitigating the risks of urban flooding. In this elevated oasis, birds find shelter, insects flourish, and plants thrive, creating a microcosm of biodiversity amidst the urban sprawl. Green roofs not only introduce nature into the city but also contribute to the preservation of local flora and fauna.

4.1.2.2 Living Walls: Aesthetic Appeal and Air Purity

Living walls, vertical gardens that grace the exteriors of buildings, redefine architectural aesthetics. These lush tapestries of greenery enhance the visual appeal of urban landscapes, providing a stark contrast to the monotony of concrete facades. Beyond their aesthetic charm, living walls play a vital role in improving air quality. Plants absorb pollutants such as carbon dioxide and release oxygen, acting as natural air purifiers. The intricate web of plants also captures particulate matter, contributing to cleaner and healthier urban air. Living walls transform buildings into vibrant canvases of life, enriching the urban environment with oxygen and beauty.

4.1.2.3 Biodiversity and Mitigating the Heat Island Effect

The introduction of green roofs and living walls ushers in biodiversity to the heart of the city. Birds, insects, and even small mammals find sanctuary within these green spaces, creating thriving ecosystems amidst the concrete surroundings. Additionally, the presence of vegetation on rooftops and building exteriors mitigates the heat island effect, where urban areas experience elevated temperatures due to human activities and heat-absorbing surfaces. By providing shade and evaporative cooling, green roofs and living walls contribute significantly to lowering temperatures, creating comfortable microclimates, and fostering an eco-friendly urban environment.

4.1.2.4 Integration into Architectural Designs: A Symphony of Nature and Architecture

Architects are embracing the concept of integrating green roofs and living walls into their designs. Innovative engineering allows for the creation of robust structures capable of supporting the weight of soil and vegetation. The strategic selection of plant species ensures compatibility with local climates and promotes biodiversity. Architects envision buildings not just as functional spaces but as living entities harmonizing with nature. Green roofs and living walls are not mere additions; they are integral components of architectural blueprints, transforming urban structures into living, breathing entities that coexist harmoniously with the natural world.

In the following sections, our exploration will extend to passive design techniques, net-zero energy buildings, and resilient urban infrastructure, painting a comprehensive portrait of sustainable urban planning and design. Each element we explore represents a vital thread in the intricate tapestry of cities that flourish in harmony with nature, nurturing vibrant communities and promising a sustainable future.

4.1.3 Passive Design Techniques:

Nature-Inspired Sustainability

Passive design techniques draw inspiration from nature, leveraging natural elements to create energy-efficient buildings. Architects study natural ventilation patterns, solar angles, and shading effects to optimize building layouts. Passive solar design captures and stores solar energy, providing heating in winter and cooling in summer. Daylight harvesting maximizes natural light, reducing the need for artificial lighting. Through these techniques, architects craft buildings that seamlessly interact with their surroundings, embracing the principles of sustainability and energy conservation.

In the quest for sustainable urban environments, architects are turning to nature as a guide, harnessing the wisdom of natural systems to craft energy-efficient buildings. Passive design techniques, inspired by the elegance of nature's processes, are at the forefront of this architectural revolution. This section immerses us in the art and science of passive design, unveiling the ingenuity with which architects optimize building layouts, capture solar energy, and utilize natural light. Through these techniques, buildings seamlessly merge with their surroundings, embracing the principles of sustainability and energy conservation.

4.1.3.1 Natural Ventilation Patterns: Breathing Life into Buildings

Architects keenly observe natural ventilation patterns to create buildings that breathe. Strategically positioned windows and vents capture prevailing winds, channeling fresh air into interior spaces. Cross-ventilation designs allow the flow of air, cooling rooms naturally and reducing the need for mechanical ventilation. By mirroring nature's airflow principles, architects craft buildings where occupants enjoy a constant supply of fresh, oxygen-rich air, fostering a healthy and comfortable indoor environment.

4.1.3.2 Solar Angles and Shading Effects: Nature's Blueprint for Comfort

Solar angles and shading effects serve as blueprints for optimizing building layouts. Architects study the path of the sun across the sky, strategically positioning windows and architectural features to harness or block sunlight. Eaves, awnings, and pergolas are meticulously designed to cast cooling shadows during the intense heat of the day, providing shelter from direct sunlight. By emulating nature's shading techniques, architects create spaces that remain naturally cool, reducing the reliance on air conditioning systems and promoting energy efficiency.

4.1.3.3 Passive Solar Design: Capturing and Storing Solar Energy

Passive solar design harnesses the abundant energy of the sun, providing heating in winter and cooling in summer. South-facing windows capture sunlight during colder months, warming interior spaces naturally. Thermal mass elements, such as concrete floors and walls, absorb and store solar heat, releasing it gradually to maintain comfortable temperatures. In summer, strategically placed overhangs and shading devices prevent excessive heat gain, ensuring that interiors remain cool. By capturing and storing solar energy passively, architects create buildings that adapt to seasonal changes, reducing the need for artificial heating and cooling systems.

4.1.3.4 Daylight Harvesting: Maximizing Nature's Illumination

Daylight harvesting maximizes the use of natural light, reducing the dependency on artificial lighting. Architects design buildings with large, strategically placed windows that allow ample daylight to penetrate interior spaces. Light shelves and reflective surfaces bounce natural light deeper into rooms, minimizing the need for electric lights during daylight hours. Sensors adjust artificial lighting levels based on the available natural light, ensuring optimal illumination while conserving energy. By embracing daylight harvesting techniques, architects create well-lit, energy-efficient spaces that enhance the well-being of occupants and minimize the environmental impact.

In the upcoming sections, our exploration will extend to net-zero energy buildings, resilient urban infrastructure, and community-centric designs, unveiling a comprehensive vision of sustainable urban planning and design. Each element we explore represents a crucial facet in the creation of cities that thrive harmoniously with nature, fostering vibrant communities and a sustainable future.

4.1.4 Net-Zero Energy Buildings:

The Future of Sustainable Architecture

Net-zero energy buildings, or NZEBs, are at the forefront of sustainable architecture. These buildings generate as much energy as they consume, balancing their energy needs through renewable sources. Solar panels, wind turbines, and geothermal systems power NZEBs, allowing them to operate off the grid or contribute excess energy back to the grid. Architects meticulously design these structures, optimizing energy usage and incorporating renewable technologies, ushering in a future where buildings not only conserve resources but actively contribute to the generation of clean energy.

In the pursuit of sustainable architecture, net-zero energy buildings (NZEBs) stand as revolutionary beacons, heralding a future where buildings not only conserve resources but actively contribute to the generation of clean energy. These buildings represent the epitome of energy efficiency, generating as much energy as they consume, thereby achieving a harmonious balance with the environment. This section immerses us in the world of NZEBs, unveiling the innovative technologies and meticulous designs that allow these structures to operate off the grid or contribute excess energy back to it. Architects, driven by a passion for sustainability, meticulously optimize energy usage and incorporate renewable technologies, ushering in a new era of architectural excellence.

4.1.4.1 Balancing Energy Needs through Renewables

NZEBs achieve energy neutrality by harnessing renewable sources. Solar panels, installed on roofs or integrated into building facades, capture the sun's energy, converting it into electricity to power the building's systems. Wind turbines, strategically positioned to harness prevailing winds, generate additional clean energy. Geothermal systems utilize the earth's natural heat, providing efficient heating and cooling for the building. By leveraging these renewable sources, NZEBs not only fulfill their energy needs sustainably but also significantly reduce the reliance on non-renewable fossil fuels, mitigating the impact on the environment.

4.1.4.2 Optimizing Energy Usage: A Meticulous Approach

Architects play a pivotal role in the design of NZEBs, meticulously optimizing energy usage. Advanced insulation materials and techniques ensure that the building retains heat in winter and remains cool in summer, reducing the demand for heating and air conditioning. Energy-efficient appliances, LED lighting, and smart thermostats further minimize electricity consumption. Passive design principles, such as strategically placed windows for natural lighting and ventilation, are seamlessly integrated, enhancing energy efficiency. Architects employ sophisticated energy modeling software to simulate various scenarios, allowing them to fine-tune the building's design for optimal performance.

4.1.4.3 Contribution to the Grid: A Surplus of Clean Energy

One of the defining features of NZEBs is their ability to contribute excess energy back to the grid. During periods of high energy generation, such as sunny days with abundant sunlight or windy conditions, NZEBs generate surplus electricity. This excess energy is fed back into the grid, offsetting the energy consumption of neighboring buildings or homes. Through net metering systems, NZEBs ensure that the clean energy they produce benefits the broader community, accelerating the transition to a renewable energy future.

4.1.4.4 Architectural Innovation and Sustainable Excellence

Architects engaged in the design of NZEBs operate at the intersection of innovation and sustainable excellence. They push the boundaries of architectural creativity while adhering to rigorous energy efficiency standards. Integrating solar panels seamlessly into the building's aesthetics, designing wind turbines as elegant sculptures, and concealing geothermal systems underground are among the innovative approaches architects employ. By marrying architectural ingenuity with sustainable technologies, architects pave the way for a future where buildings not only serve as functional spaces but also as symbols of environmental stewardship and visionary design.

In the subsequent sections, our exploration will extend to resilient urban infrastructure, community-centric designs, and innovative transportation systems, painting a comprehensive portrait of sustainable urban planning and design. Each element we explore represents a vital thread in the intricate tapestry of cities that flourish harmoniously with nature, fostering vibrant communities and promising a sustainable future.

In the subsequent sections, we will explore urban green spaces, community-centric designs, and resilient infrastructure, unveiling a comprehensive vision of sustainable urban planning and design. Each element contributes to the creation of cities that thrive in harmony with nature, fostering vibrant communities and a sustainable future.

Section 4.2: Renewable Energy Solutions

In the pursuit of sustainable urban environments, the integration of renewable energy sources has emerged as a fundamental pillar. This section delves into the implementation of renewable energy solutions, focusing on harnessing the power of solar, wind, and geothermal energy in the heart of urban landscapes. By embracing these clean and renewable sources, cities are not only reducing their carbon footprint but also paving the way for a future where clean energy powers the entirety of urban life.

4.2.1 Solar Energy: Harnessing the Power of the Sun

Solar energy, abundant and infinitely renewable, serves as a cornerstone of urban sustainability. Photovoltaic panels, installed on rooftops, facades, and even integrated into urban infrastructure, capture sunlight and convert it into electricity. Solar farms located on the outskirts of cities harness vast expanses of land to generate clean energy on a larger scale. Smart grids and energy storage systems ensure that solar energy is efficiently distributed and utilized, providing power for homes, businesses, and public facilities. The proliferation of solar energy not only reduces dependence on fossil fuels but also empowers communities to harness the sun's energy for a myriad of applications, from street lighting to powering electric vehicles.

4.2.2 Wind Energy: Tapping into the Power of the Breeze

Wind energy, harnessed through wind turbines strategically positioned in urban areas and wind farms in nearby regions, captures the kinetic energy of the wind and transforms it into electricity. Urban wind turbines, designed to complement the architectural aesthetics, are integrated into the cityscape, providing a local source of clean energy. Wind farms, located in proximity to cities, tap into the consistent winds of open landscapes, generating significant amounts of electricity. The synergy between urban and rural wind energy production ensures a sustainable and continuous supply of wind power, contributing to the city's energy grid and reducing reliance on non-renewable sources.

4.2.3 Geothermal Energy: Tapping into Earth's Natural Heat

Geothermal energy, harnessed from the natural heat of the Earth's crust, offers a reliable and renewable source of power for urban environments. Geothermal power plants utilize underground reservoirs of steam and hot water to drive turbines and generate electricity. In urban areas, geothermal heat pumps are installed beneath buildings, utilizing the Earth's stable temperature to provide heating in winter and cooling in summer. The implementation of geothermal energy systems not only reduces greenhouse gas emissions but also enhances energy efficiency, making cities more resilient and sustainable in the face of fluctuating energy demands.

4.2.4 Integration and Urban Sustainability

The seamless integration of solar, wind, and geothermal energy sources into urban environments embodies the essence of sustainable urban planning. Architects and engineers collaborate to design buildings with integrated solar panels, ensuring that new constructions generate their own clean energy. Wind turbines, strategically placed in parks and green spaces, contribute to the city's renewable energy mix while becoming iconic symbols of sustainable living. Geothermal heat pumps, hidden beneath urban developments, provide reliable heating and cooling, reducing the burden on traditional HVAC systems. The comprehensive integration of these renewable sources transforms cities into self-sufficient energy hubs, setting the stage for a future where urban areas are powered entirely by renewable energy.

In the upcoming sections, our exploration will extend to resilient urban infrastructure, community-centric designs, and innovative transportation systems, painting a comprehensive portrait of sustainable urban planning and design. Each element we explore represents a vital thread in the intricate tapestry of cities that flourish harmoniously with nature, fostering vibrant communities and promising a sustainable future.

Section 4.3: Waste Management and Recycling

Effective waste management systems, innovative recycling initiatives, and the implementation of circular economy models stand as cornerstones of progressive cities striving for sustainability. This section delves into the intricate web of waste management and recycling, examining how forward-thinking urban centers have embraced sustainable practices to minimize waste, promote recycling, and create a circular economy where resources are conserved, reused, and recycled, fostering environmental stewardship and economic resilience.

4.3.1 Effective Waste Management Systems: From Collection to Disposal

Progressive cities employ advanced waste management systems that prioritize efficiency and environmental consciousness. Thoughtful waste collection strategies, utilizing segregated bins for recyclables and organic waste, ensure proper sorting at the source. Efficient transportation networks then transport waste to state-of-the-art recycling facilities and landfill sites. These cities invest in cutting-edge waste-to-energy technologies, converting non-recyclable waste into clean energy, reducing the burden on landfills, and mitigating environmental impact. By optimizing waste management processes, cities minimize pollution, conserve valuable land, and move closer to a zero-waste future.

4.3.2 Recycling Initiatives: Transforming Waste into Resources

Recycling initiatives in progressive cities extend far beyond basic paper and plastic recycling. These cities embrace comprehensive recycling programs that encompass electronics, textiles, and even construction materials. Recycling centers equipped with state-of-the-art machinery sort and process recyclable materials efficiently. Public awareness campaigns educate citizens about the importance of recycling and encourage active participation. Additionally, cities incentivize recycling through reward programs and tax benefits, motivating businesses and individuals alike to engage in responsible waste disposal practices. By transforming waste into valuable resources, cities contribute to the conservation of raw materials, energy savings, and the reduction of greenhouse gas emissions.

4.3.3 Circular Economy Models: Redefining Resource Consumption

Circular economy models represent a paradigm shift in how cities approach resource consumption. Instead of the traditional linear model of take, make, and dispose, circular economies prioritize reducing, reusing, and recycling. Cities at the forefront of sustainability embrace circular economy principles, encouraging businesses to design products with recyclability in mind and fostering collaborations between industries to exchange waste materials as resources. Circular supply chains are established, ensuring that products and materials have a second life through recycling or repurposing. By closing the loop and minimizing waste, cities create a resilient and sustainable economic system where resources are continuously cycled, reducing environmental impact and promoting long-term environmental and economic stability.

4.3.4 Community Engagement and Sustainability Education

Central to the success of waste management and recycling initiatives is community engagement and sustainability education. Progressive cities prioritize educating citizens about waste reduction, recycling, and the principles of circular economies. Schools, community centers, and online platforms host workshops and awareness campaigns, fostering a culture of environmental responsibility. Citizens are encouraged to participate in clean-up drives, recycling events, and neighborhood composting programs. By empowering communities with knowledge and encouraging active involvement, cities not only enhance the effectiveness of their waste management systems but also nurture a sense of collective responsibility, creating a sustainable legacy for future generations.

In the upcoming sections, our exploration will extend to resilient urban infrastructure, community-centric designs, and innovative transportation systems, painting a comprehensive portrait of sustainable urban planning and design. Each element we explore represents a vital thread in the intricate tapestry of cities that flourish harmoniously with nature, fostering vibrant communities and promising a sustainable future.

Chapter 5: Smart Infrastructure and Technology

Section 5.1: Smart Grids and Energy Management

In the age of smart infrastructure, cities are embracing innovative technologies to revolutionize the way energy is generated, distributed, and consumed. Smart grids and advanced energy management systems lie at the heart of this transformation, offering dynamic solutions to optimize energy usage, enhance grid reliability, and mitigate environmental impact. This section delves into the intricate world of smart grids and energy management, examining how these cutting-edge technologies enable cities to achieve unprecedented levels of efficiency, sustainability, and environmental stewardship.

5.1.1 Smart Grids: The Backbone of Sustainable Energy

Smart grids represent a paradigm shift in the energy landscape, integrating digital communication and advanced sensors into the traditional electricity grid. These intelligent networks enable real-time monitoring of energy production, consumption, and distribution. Smart grids automatically detect and respond to changes in demand, rerouting electricity to where it is needed most efficiently. They incorporate renewable energy sources seamlessly, balancing the intermittent nature of solar and wind power. By optimizing the flow of electricity, reducing transmission losses, and enhancing grid resilience, smart grids pave the way for a reliable, flexible, and sustainable energy future.

5.1.2 Advanced Energy Management Systems: Precision in Power Consumption

Advanced energy management systems empower cities, businesses, and households with unprecedented control over their energy usage. Smart meters provide real-time data on electricity consumption, allowing consumers to make informed decisions about their usage patterns. Demand response programs enable businesses to adjust their energy usage during peak demand periods, reducing strain on the grid and avoiding the need for additional power plants. Machine learning algorithms analyze historical consumption data, predicting future demand patterns and optimizing energy distribution. Through precise monitoring, analysis, and control, advanced energy management systems minimize waste, lower costs, and significantly reduce the environmental footprint associated with energy production.

5.1.3 Integration of Renewable Energy Sources: A Greener Grid

Smart grids and advanced energy management systems seamlessly integrate renewable energy sources into the energy mix. Solar panels, wind turbines, and other renewable installations feed clean energy into the grid. Advanced forecasting algorithms predict renewable energy generation patterns, allowing grid operators to balance supply and demand effectively. Energy storage systems, such as advanced batteries, store excess renewable energy for use during periods of high demand or low generation. By harnessing the power of renewables and ensuring their smooth integration into the grid, cities reduce their reliance on fossil fuels, lower greenhouse gas emissions, and accelerate the transition to a sustainable energy ecosystem.

5.1.4 Grid Resilience and Disaster Preparedness

Smart grids enhance grid resilience and disaster preparedness, ensuring continuity of service even in challenging circumstances. Advanced sensors detect faults and outages instantly, enabling rapid response teams to identify and address issues swiftly. Smart grids can reroute electricity, isolating affected areas and preventing cascading failures. In the event of natural disasters, microgrids—localized, self-sufficient energy networks—can operate independently, providing critical services to emergency facilities. By enhancing grid resilience, smart grids bolster cities' ability to withstand disruptions, recover quickly, and provide essential services to residents, reinforcing their role as resilient, sustainable urban centers.

Section 5.2: IoT in Urban Services

The integration of the Internet of Things (IoT) into urban services marks a pivotal advancement in smart infrastructure. This section delves into the multifaceted applications of IoT in urban environments, revolutionizing essential services and fostering unparalleled levels of efficiency, responsiveness, and sustainability. From optimizing transportation networks to revolutionizing waste management and enhancing public safety, IoT technologies are reshaping cities, creating connected, intelligent, and safer urban spaces.

5.2.1 Smart Transportation: Navigating Cities Efficiently

In the realm of smart transportation, IoT technologies are revolutionizing the way cities move. Connected vehicles equipped with sensors communicate real-time data to centralized traffic management systems. These systems analyze traffic patterns, predict congestion, and dynamically adjust traffic signals to optimize flow. Smart parking solutions guide drivers to available parking spaces, reducing traffic congestion and emissions caused by circling vehicles. IoT-enabled public transportation systems provide real-time updates on bus and train schedules, enhancing reliability and passenger experience. By harnessing IoT, cities create seamless, efficient transportation networks, reducing travel times, minimizing congestion, and promoting the use of public transit.

5.2.2 Intelligent Waste Management: From Collection to Recycling

IoT applications in waste management transform traditional systems into intelligent, data-driven processes. Smart bins equipped with sensors monitor fill levels, alerting waste collection teams when bins are ready for emptying. Route optimization algorithms analyze data from sensors, determining the most efficient collection routes to reduce fuel consumption and operational costs. Recycling stations equipped with IoT sensors sort recyclables automatically, enhancing recycling rates and reducing contamination. Smart waste management not only minimizes operational costs but also promotes sustainability by encouraging recycling, reducing landfill waste, and conserving valuable resources.

5.2.3 IoT in Public Safety: Enhancing Security and Emergency Response

In the realm of public safety, IoT technologies bolster security measures and enhance emergency response capabilities. Smart surveillance systems equipped with sensors and facial recognition technology monitor public spaces, detecting anomalies and potential security threats. Connected emergency response systems receive real-time data from various sources, allowing rapid deployment of resources during accidents, natural disasters, or incidents. IoT-enabled wearable devices, such as smart helmets for firefighters or health monitors for police officers, provide critical data to commanders, ensuring the well-being and safety of first responders. By leveraging IoT in public safety, cities enhance their ability to prevent, respond to, and recover from emergencies, creating safer environments for residents and visitors alike.

5.2.4 Environmental Monitoring and Sustainability

IoT applications extend to environmental monitoring, enabling cities to track air quality, noise pollution, and other environmental parameters in real time. Sensors deployed throughout the city collect data, which is analyzed to identify pollution sources and trends. Smart irrigation systems utilize IoT sensors to monitor soil moisture levels, optimizing water usage for urban green spaces. Environmental monitoring data informs city planning, enabling the implementation of policies to reduce pollution and conserve resources. By harnessing IoT for environmental sustainability, cities take proactive measures to protect natural habitats, improve air quality, and create healthier, more livable environments for residents.

Section 5.3: Data-Driven Urban Decision Making

In the era of smart cities, data has become a powerful catalyst for informed decision-making, transforming urban governance into a dynamic and responsive process. This section delves into the transformative impact of data analytics and artificial intelligence on urban decision making, exploring how cities leverage vast streams of data to gain insights, optimize services, and enhance the overall quality of life for their residents. From predictive modeling to citizen engagement, data-driven urban governance represents a paradigm shift, fostering efficient, transparent, and citizen-centric cities.

5.3.1 Predictive Analytics: Anticipating Urban Needs

Predictive analytics algorithms sift through vast datasets, identifying patterns and trends that empower city planners and policymakers to anticipate urban needs. These algorithms forecast traffic congestion, enabling dynamic traffic management and rerouting. Predictive maintenance models anticipate infrastructure wear and tear, optimizing repairs and minimizing disruptions. Public service demands, from waste collection to healthcare, are predicted, allowing cities to allocate resources efficiently. By harnessing predictive analytics, cities transform reactive decision-making into proactive strategies, mitigating issues before they escalate and enhancing the overall urban experience.

5.3.2 Citizen Engagement and Participatory Governance

Data-driven urban decision making extends to citizen engagement, creating avenues for residents to actively participate in governance. Online platforms and mobile applications enable citizens to report issues, offer suggestions, and engage in virtual town hall meetings. Sentiment analysis algorithms parse through social media feeds and online forums, gauging public opinions and concerns. Citizen-generated data becomes a valuable resource, guiding policy formulation and service delivery. Participatory budgeting, enabled by data analytics, allows citizens to influence budget allocation based on their priorities. Through these mechanisms, cities foster a sense of community ownership, transparency, and collaborative decision-making.

5.3.3 AI-Driven Urban Planning: Optimizing City Layouts

Artificial intelligence (AI) algorithms are revolutionizing urban planning, optimizing city layouts for efficiency and sustainability. Machine learning models analyze urban mobility patterns, informing the development of efficient public transportation routes and bike-sharing programs. AI-driven simulations evaluate the environmental impact of construction projects, ensuring eco-friendly designs. Smart zoning algorithms optimize land use, balancing residential, commercial, and green spaces. AI-powered urban planning not only streamlines processes but also fosters harmonious, well-balanced urban environments, enhancing quality of life and preserving natural resources.

5.3.4 Data Security and Ethical Considerations

Amidst the data-driven transformation, ensuring data security and ethical considerations are paramount. Cities invest in robust cybersecurity measures to safeguard citizen data, employing encryption, secure cloud storage, and regular vulnerability assessments. Ethical guidelines and regulations govern the collection, storage, and use of citizen data, ensuring privacy and consent. Transparent data usage policies are communicated to citizens, fostering trust in the urban governance process. By upholding data security and ethical standards, cities create a foundation of trust, essential for the success of data-driven urban decision making.

In the subsequent sections, our exploration will extend to digital infrastructure, IoT-driven urban evolution, and the holistic vision of smart cities, painting a comprehensive portrait of the interconnected, intelligent urban environments of tomorrow. Each element we explore represents a vital thread in the intricate tapestry of cities that leverage data analytics and artificial intelligence to empower citizens, enhance governance, and create vibrant, sustainable urban landscapes.

Chapter 6: Green Spaces and Biodiversity

Section 6.1: Urban Farming and Food Security

In the pursuit of sustainable urban living, cities are turning to innovative solutions to address food security, promote local agriculture, and reduce the carbon footprint. Urban farming initiatives have emerged as a transformative force, reshaping urban landscapes and fostering a deeper connection between city dwellers and their food sources. This section delves into the world of urban farming, exploring its multifaceted benefits and the pivotal role it plays in creating resilient, self-sufficient cities.

6.1.1 Rooftop Gardens and Vertical Farming: Cultivating Upwards

Rooftop gardens and vertical farming systems epitomize the integration of agriculture into urban spaces. Rooftop gardens utilize the unused spaces atop buildings, transforming them into lush havens for crops. Vertical farming takes this concept to new heights, literally, by cultivating crops in stacked layers within specialized indoor facilities. These methods maximize space efficiency, allowing cities to produce a diverse array of crops in a limited footprint. Through innovative techniques such as hydroponics and aquaponics, urban farmers optimize water usage while eliminating the need for harmful pesticides, creating a sustainable and organic approach to food cultivation.

6.1.2 Community Gardens: Fostering Social Cohesion

Community gardens serve as vibrant hubs of social interaction and agricultural activity. These shared spaces are tended to by community members, fostering a sense of ownership and pride. In addition to providing fresh produce, community gardens offer educational opportunities, teaching residents about agriculture, nutrition, and environmental stewardship. The collaborative atmosphere promotes social cohesion and a sense of community, as neighbors work together to nurture their shared green spaces. Community gardens become focal points for workshops, educational events, and cultural exchanges, enriching the social fabric of neighborhoods.

6.1.3 Local Agriculture and Farmer's Markets: Connecting Producers and Consumers

The resurgence of local agriculture and farmer's markets revitalizes the connection between producers and consumers. Local farmers bring fresh, seasonal produce directly to urban centers, reducing the carbon footprint associated with long-distance transportation. Consumers have the opportunity to engage with the people who grow their food, learning about cultivation methods and the benefits of locally sourced produce. By supporting local agriculture, cities stimulate the regional economy, preserve agricultural landscapes, and ensure a diverse and sustainable food supply for urban populations.

6.1.4 Food Security and Climate Resilience

Urban farming plays a vital role in enhancing food security and climate resilience. By diversifying the sources of fresh produce, cities reduce their dependence on centralized, vulnerable food supply chains. In the face of climate change, where traditional agricultural practices might be threatened by extreme weather events, urban farming offers a resilient alternative. Indoor farming facilities provide a controlled environment, shielding crops from adverse weather conditions. Additionally, the cultivation of diverse crops promotes biodiversity, making urban agriculture more resilient to pests and diseases. By bolstering food security and climate resilience, cities create a foundation for sustainable living, ensuring that residents have access to nutritious food regardless of external challenges.

In the subsequent sections, our exploration will extend to the preservation of natural habitats, urban reforestation efforts, and the integration of green spaces into urban planning, painting a comprehensive portrait of cities that harmonize with nature, fostering vibrant communities and promising a sustainable future.

Section 6.2: Preserving Natural Habitats

Preserving natural habitats within urban environments is essential for maintaining biodiversity, supporting native flora and fauna, and creating spaces for residents to connect with nature. This section explores the significance of preserving natural habitats in the midst of urban development and the various strategies cities employ to conserve these vital ecosystems.

6.2.1 Urban Parks and Wildlife Sanctuaries: Oasis of Biodiversity

Urban parks and wildlife sanctuaries serve as havens for biodiversity in the heart of bustling cities. These protected areas provide habitats for native plants and animals, creating a balanced ecosystem within urban landscapes. Cities design these spaces with care, incorporating diverse plant species that attract pollinators and creating water features that support aquatic life. Wildlife sanctuaries, in particular, provide refuge for migratory birds and endangered species. By preserving these natural habitats, cities offer residents the opportunity to observe and appreciate wildlife, fostering a deep connection with the natural world.

6.2.2 Green Corridors and Biodiversity Pathways: Connecting Habitats

Green corridors and biodiversity pathways are essential for connecting fragmented habitats within urban areas. These green routes allow wildlife to move between parks, forests, and water bodies, promoting genetic diversity and preventing inbreeding. Cities strategically plan these corridors, planting native trees and creating undisturbed areas to facilitate the movement of animals. Additionally, green corridors enhance the overall green cover of the city, mitigating the urban heat island effect and improving air quality. By creating interconnected pathways for wildlife, cities support diverse ecosystems and contribute to the overall health of the environment.

6.2.3 Native Plant Landscaping: Promoting Biodiversity

Cities promote biodiversity by encouraging the use of native plants in landscaping projects. Native plant species are adapted to the local climate and soil conditions, requiring less water and maintenance than non-native species. Municipalities incentivize property owners and businesses to incorporate native plants in gardens and public spaces. This approach not only supports local biodiversity but also creates vibrant, colorful landscapes that enhance the aesthetic appeal of the city. Moreover, native plant landscaping attracts native insects and birds, creating a thriving ecosystem within urban areas.

6.2.4 Citizen Engagement in Habitat Preservation: Stewardship of Nature

Citizen engagement plays a vital role in habitat preservation efforts. Cities organize volunteer programs, educational workshops, and community events to raise awareness about the importance of preserving natural habitats. Residents actively participate in tree planting initiatives, habitat restoration projects, and ecological surveys. Citizen scientists contribute valuable data on local flora and fauna, aiding conservation efforts. By involving the community in habitat preservation, cities create a sense of shared responsibility, fostering a culture of environmental stewardship that transcends generations.

Section 6.3: Green Roofs and Vertical Gardens

Discuss the implementation of green roofs and vertical gardens in urban spaces to enhance biodiversity and improve air quality.

Green roofs and vertical gardens represent innovative solutions to enhance urban biodiversity and air quality. By transforming conventional rooftops and vertical surfaces into thriving ecosystems, cities can create sustainable environments that benefit both nature and residents.

6.3.1 Green Roofs: Rooftop Oases of Biodiversity

Green roofs, adorned with a variety of plant species, serve as rooftop oases of biodiversity. These living roofs not only provide insulation, reducing energy consumption, but also offer habitats for birds, insects, and even small mammals. Native and drought-resistant plants are carefully selected to create resilient ecosystems that attract pollinators and support local fauna. Green roofs act as natural filters, purifying rainwater and reducing stormwater runoff. By implementing green roofs, cities enhance biodiversity, mitigate the urban heat island effect, and contribute to the overall ecological health of urban areas.

6.3.2 Vertical Gardens: Green Walls Breathing Life

Vertical gardens, or green walls, transform barren walls into lush, green surfaces. These structures utilize a variety of plants, from vines to ferns, creating vertical habitats for insects and birds. Green walls improve air quality by absorbing carbon dioxide and releasing oxygen, making urban environments healthier for residents. Additionally, vertical gardens provide insulation, reducing indoor temperatures and lowering energy costs. By incorporating vertical gardens into urban architecture, cities maximize green spaces, create visually appealing environments, and foster biodiversity in unexpected places.

6.3.3 Ecological Benefits and Community Engagement

The implementation of green roofs and vertical gardens yields numerous ecological benefits. These installations help reduce air pollution by capturing particulate matter and absorbing pollutants. They also act as sound barriers, dampening noise pollution in busy urban areas. Furthermore, green roofs and vertical gardens serve as educational tools, engaging communities in workshops and demonstrations about sustainable living and urban ecology. Residents actively participate in the maintenance of these green spaces, fostering a sense of pride and ownership. By combining ecological benefits with community engagement, cities create harmonious, nature-integrated urban environments that promote the well-being of both residents and the planet.

Section 6.4: Biodiversity Conservation Efforts

Urban areas are not exempt from the global biodiversity crisis. As cities expand, conservation efforts become paramount to preserve the diverse flora and fauna that call these areas home. This section delves into the dedicated conservation projects and initiatives that cities implement to protect urban biodiversity. From creating wildlife habitats to establishing green corridors, cities are taking proactive measures to ensure the coexistence of nature and urban development.

6.3.1 Wildlife Habitats: Urban Sanctuaries for Fauna

Cities establish designated wildlife habitats within urban spaces to provide refuge for native animals. These habitats mimic natural ecosystems, incorporating features such as ponds, nesting sites, and indigenous plant species. Wildlife habitats support various species, from birds and insects to small mammals and amphibians. By creating these sanctuaries, cities safeguard biodiversity, allowing urban residents to observe and appreciate the richness of local wildlife. Educational programs often accompany these habitats, enlightening citizens about the importance of coexisting with the diverse animal species that share their urban environment.

6.3.2 Green Corridors: Lifelines for Biodiversity

Green corridors serve as lifelines for urban biodiversity, connecting fragmented habitats and allowing wildlife to move freely between them. These corridors are carefully planned strips of greenery that link parks, gardens, and natural reserves. Cities plant native trees, shrubs, and wildflowers along these pathways, creating an uninterrupted natural route for animals. Green corridors enhance genetic diversity by facilitating the movement of species, reducing the risks associated with inbreeding. Additionally, these corridors act as natural carbon sinks, absorbing carbon dioxide and mitigating the effects of climate change. By establishing green corridors, cities ensure the long-term survival of their diverse flora and fauna.

6.3.3 Citizen Involvement: Guardians of Biodiversity

Engaging citizens in biodiversity conservation efforts is essential for the success of these initiatives. Cities organize volunteer programs, citizen science projects, and workshops to involve residents in hands-on conservation activities. Citizens participate in tree planting, bird watching, and ecological surveys, contributing valuable data to conservation research. Educational campaigns raise awareness about the importance of preserving urban biodiversity, encouraging residents to create wildlife-friendly spaces in their own gardens. By nurturing a sense of stewardship among citizens, cities create a network of guardians dedicated to protecting the natural heritage of their urban environment.

6.3.4 Collaboration and Research: Partnerships for Biodiversity

Cities collaborate with environmental organizations, research institutions, and local communities to enhance biodiversity conservation efforts. Joint research projects provide valuable insights into urban ecosystems, guiding conservation strategies. Partnerships with schools and universities foster environmental education and awareness among the younger generation. By pooling resources and knowledge, cities create a comprehensive approach to biodiversity conservation, ensuring that conservation efforts are grounded in scientific research and community involvement.

In the subsequent sections, our exploration will extend to sustainable urban planning, resilient infrastructure, and the holistic vision of eco-friendly cities, painting a comprehensive portrait of cities that harmonize with nature, fostering vibrant communities and promising a sustainable future.

Chapter 7: Mobility and Transportation Solutions

Section 7.1: Autonomous Vehicles and Future of Transportation

Urban transportation stands on the cusp of a revolutionary transformation with the advent of autonomous vehicles. This section delves into the cutting-edge advancements in self-driving technology and explores the profound impact these innovations have on urban mobility. From enhancing safety to mitigating traffic congestion, autonomous vehicles represent a paradigm shift in the way cities approach transportation, promising a future where mobility is not only efficient but also environmentally sustainable.

7.1.1 The Rise of Autonomous Vehicles: A Technological Revolution

Autonomous vehicles, equipped with advanced sensors, artificial intelligence, and machine learning algorithms, are heralding a new era in transportation. These self-driving cars, buses, and even drones have the ability to perceive their surroundings, navigate complex traffic scenarios, and make split-second decisions. The integration of real-time data, including traffic patterns and pedestrian movement, enables these vehicles to optimize routes, ensuring efficient and safe travel. The rapid advancements in autonomous technology are reshaping the landscape of urban mobility, paving the way for a future where transportation is not only driverless but also highly intelligent and responsive.

7.1.2 Enhancing Safety: Redefining Urban Transport Security

One of the key advantages of autonomous vehicles is their potential to significantly enhance road safety. Self-driving cars are not susceptible to human errors such as fatigue, distraction, or impaired judgment, which are leading causes of accidents. Advanced sensors, including lidar and cameras, provide a 360-degree view of the vehicle's surroundings, detecting obstacles and pedestrians with precision. Machine learning algorithms enable these vehicles to predict and respond to potential collisions in real-time, reducing the likelihood of accidents. By minimizing accidents and improving overall road safety, autonomous vehicles create a safer urban environment for both drivers and pedestrians.

7.1.3 Mitigating Traffic Congestion: Smoothing the Urban Flow

Traffic congestion is a ubiquitous challenge in urban areas, leading to wasted time, increased pollution, and decreased productivity. Autonomous vehicles have the potential to mitigate congestion by optimizing traffic flow and reducing bottlenecks. Through vehicle-to-vehicle

(V2V) and vehicle-to-infrastructure (V2I) communication, self-driving cars can coordinate movements, preventing sudden stops and starts that often lead to traffic jams. Intelligent traffic management systems analyze real-time data from autonomous vehicles, adjusting traffic signals and routes dynamically to ensure the smooth flow of traffic. By reducing congestion, autonomous vehicles not only save time for commuters but also decrease fuel consumption and greenhouse gas emissions, contributing to a more sustainable urban ecosystem.

7.1.4 Accessibility and Inclusivity: Transportation for All

Autonomous vehicles have the potential to revolutionize transportation accessibility, particularly for individuals with disabilities and the elderly. Self-driving cars can be equipped with specialized features such as ramps and automated boarding systems, making them accessible to wheelchair users and people with mobility challenges. Moreover, autonomous vehicles offer a convenient and reliable transportation option for the elderly, providing them with increased independence and mobility. By ensuring inclusivity in urban transportation, self-driving technology enhances the overall quality of life for diverse populations, fostering a more equitable and accessible city for all residents.

In the subsequent sections, our exploration will extend to sustainable transportation infrastructure, shared mobility solutions, and the integration of technology in public transit, painting a comprehensive portrait of cities that prioritize efficient, safe, and accessible urban mobility, promising a future where transportation is seamless and sustainable.

Section 7.2: Hyperloop and High-Speed Rail Systems

Discuss futuristic transportation concepts like Hyperloop and high-speed rail networks, examining their feasibility, benefits, and potential impact on urban mobility.

The future of urban mobility is being reshaped by revolutionary concepts such as Hyperloop and high-speed rail systems. This section delves into these futuristic transportation technologies, exploring their feasibility, benefits, and potential impact on urban mobility. From blistering speeds to environmental sustainability, these innovations promise to transform the way people travel, connecting cities in unprecedented ways and offering a glimpse into a high-speed, interconnected future.

7.2.1 Hyperloop: Speeding Through Tubes

Hyperloop, a visionary transportation concept, envisions passenger pods traveling at near-supersonic speeds through low-pressure tubes. Propelled by magnetic levitation and propelled by linear induction motors, Hyperloop pods have the potential to reach speeds of up to 700 miles per hour (1,100 kilometers per hour). This remarkable velocity could drastically reduce travel times between cities, turning hours-long journeys into mere minutes. By eliminating friction and air resistance, Hyperloop not only offers unparalleled speed but also energy efficiency, making it a promising solution for long-distance, high-speed urban transportation.

7.2.2 High-Speed Rail Networks: Bridging Cities with Speed and Efficiency

High-speed rail systems, already operational in several countries, connect cities with trains traveling at speeds exceeding 155 miles per hour (250 kilometers per hour). These networks offer a swift and convenient alternative to air travel for medium to long distances. High-speed trains are not only energy-efficient but also produce fewer emissions per passenger compared to traditional cars and airplanes. The development of high-speed rail networks promotes regional integration, boosts local economies, and reduces congestion on roads and at airports. Additionally, these systems enhance connectivity, fostering cultural and economic exchange between cities.

7.2.3 Feasibility and Challenges: Building the Future of Transportation

While the potential benefits of Hyperloop and high-speed rail systems are immense, their implementation comes with challenges. Constructing the necessary infrastructure, including specialized tracks and low-pressure tubes for Hyperloop, requires significant investment and meticulous planning. Environmental considerations, land acquisition, and regulatory approvals are critical aspects that need to be addressed. Furthermore, ensuring the safety and security of passengers at such high speeds demands cutting-edge technology and rigorous testing. Despite these challenges, ongoing research and development in the field of transportation engineering are gradually overcoming these hurdles, bringing the dream of high-speed urban mobility closer to reality.

7.2.4 Environmental Impact and Sustainability: Paving the Green Path

One of the key advantages of high-speed rail systems and Hyperloop is their environmental sustainability. By offering an eco-friendly alternative to air travel and traditional cars, these transportation modes contribute to reducing greenhouse gas emissions and mitigating climate change. High-speed trains, powered by electricity, have a lower carbon footprint per passenger kilometer than most other modes of transport. Additionally, the potential integration of renewable energy sources further enhances the environmental sustainability of these transportation systems. By prioritizing clean energy and green technology, Hyperloop and high-speed rail networks represent a significant step toward creating sustainable urban transportation networks.

In the subsequent sections, our exploration will extend to innovative urban mobility solutions, smart transportation infrastructure, and the seamless integration of various transportation modes, painting a comprehensive portrait of cities that prioritize efficiency, sustainability, and interconnected mobility, promising a future where travel is not just rapid but also environmentally conscious.

Section 7.3: Sustainable Public Transportation

Examine eco-friendly public transportation systems, including electric buses, trams, and subways, and their role in reducing emissions and promoting sustainable urban living.

In the pursuit of sustainable urban living, cities are turning towards eco-friendly public transportation systems as a cornerstone of their mobility strategies. This section delves into the realm of sustainable public transportation, examining the pivotal role played by electric buses, trams, and subways in reducing emissions and fostering environmentally conscious urban living. From zero-emission vehicles to energy-efficient infrastructures, these systems showcase a commitment to a greener future, transforming the way people commute and enhancing the overall quality of urban life.

7.3.1 Electric Buses: Navigating the Green Route

Electric buses have emerged as a promising solution to reduce emissions and noise pollution in urban areas. These buses, powered by electricity stored in advanced batteries, produce zero tailpipe emissions, making them environmentally friendly alternatives to traditional diesel buses. With advancements in battery technology, electric buses offer extended ranges and shorter charging times, ensuring seamless operation throughout the day. Cities are increasingly adopting electric buses into their public transportation fleets, promoting cleaner air and a healthier urban environment for both passengers and pedestrians.

7.3.2 Trams: A Sustainable Commuting Option

Trams, or streetcars, represent a sustainable and efficient mode of public transportation. These electric-powered vehicles run on tracks embedded in city streets, offering a smooth and reliable commuting experience. Trams produce zero emissions at the point of use, making them environmentally friendly alternatives for densely populated urban areas. By providing dedicated tram lanes and priority at traffic signals, cities optimize tram networks, reducing travel times and encouraging more people to choose public transportation over private cars. Trams not only promote sustainable urban mobility but also contribute to the reduction of traffic congestion and greenhouse gas emissions.

7.3.3 Subways: The Underground Green Corridors

Subway systems, operating underground, provide efficient and eco-friendly transportation options for urban residents. Electric-powered trains produce no direct emissions, making subways one of the most environmentally sustainable modes of mass transit. The integration of regenerative braking systems further enhances energy efficiency, capturing and reusing energy during deceleration. Subways not only reduce traffic congestion on the surface but also minimize air pollution and noise levels in densely populated areas. By investing in expanding and modernizing subway networks, cities create underground green corridors that facilitate smooth, rapid, and sustainable commuting for millions of residents.

7.3.4 Integration and Accessibility: A Holistic Approach

The key to a truly sustainable public transportation system lies in integration and accessibility. Cities are investing in comprehensive networks that seamlessly connect buses, trams, subways, and other modes of transport. Integrated ticketing systems and real-time passenger information ensure convenience and efficiency for commuters. Moreover, cities are actively promoting accessibility, ensuring that public transportation is inclusive for people with disabilities and the elderly. By adopting a holistic approach that considers integration, accessibility, and environmental impact, cities create public transportation systems that not only reduce emissions but also enhance the overall urban experience for diverse populations.

Chapter 8: Social Inclusion and Community Engagement

Section 8.1: Affordable Housing Solutions

Explore innovative approaches to affordable housing, including cooperative housing models, micro-housing, and community land trusts, ensuring housing accessibility for all.

Accessible and affordable housing is the bedrock of inclusive and thriving communities. This section delves into innovative approaches to affordable housing, exploring diverse models such as cooperative housing, micro-housing, and community land trusts. By ensuring housing affordability and accessibility for all residents, cities foster social inclusion and empower communities, creating a foundation for vibrant and equitable urban living.

8.1.1 Cooperative Housing: Building Communities Together

Cooperative housing models empower residents by allowing them to collectively own and manage their housing complexes. In these communities, residents pool resources to purchase and maintain properties, ensuring affordability and stability. Cooperative housing fosters a sense of community and shared responsibility, creating a supportive environment where residents actively participate in decision-making processes. By promoting collaboration and mutual support, cooperative housing models provide affordable homes while nurturing strong social bonds among residents.

8.1.2 Micro-Housing: Compact Living, Big Impact

Micro-housing, characterized by compact living spaces that maximize functionality, represents an innovative solution to housing affordability challenges. These small, efficiently designed units are equipped with space-saving features and smart technology, enabling residents to make the most of limited square footage. Micro-housing developments often incorporate shared amenities and communal spaces, encouraging social interaction among residents. By embracing minimalist living and efficient design, micro-housing provides affordable housing options for individuals and small families, promoting sustainability and community living.

8.1.3 Community Land Trusts: Preserving Affordable Housing

Community land trusts (CLTs) are nonprofit organizations that acquire and hold land for the benefit of the community. Through CLTs, housing remains permanently affordable, as the land is owned collectively while the housing units are owned individually. This model ensures that homes remain accessible for future generations, preventing gentrification and displacement. CLTs empower residents by giving them control over the use and development of land, fostering a sense of community ownership. By preserving affordable housing in perpetuity, CLTs create stable neighborhoods where residents can invest in their homes and communities without the fear of escalating costs.

8.1.4 Green Affordable Housing: Sustainable Living for All

Green affordable housing integrates environmentally sustainable features into affordable housing developments. These features include energy-efficient appliances, renewable energy sources, rainwater harvesting systems, and eco-friendly building materials. By reducing energy consumption and minimizing environmental impact, green affordable housing not only lowers utility costs for residents but also contributes to a healthier environment. Sustainable landscaping and green spaces further enhance the quality of life for residents. By combining affordability with environmental consciousness, cities create housing solutions that prioritize both the well-being of residents and the planet.

In the subsequent sections, our exploration will extend to social inclusion initiatives, community engagement programs, and the integration of diverse populations into urban planning, painting a comprehensive portrait of cities that prioritize affordable housing, social equity, and community engagement, promising a future where every resident has a place to call home and a sense of belonging in their community.

Section 8.2: Accessible Public Spaces and Inclusive Design

Discuss the importance of inclusive urban design, focusing on accessible public spaces, buildings, and infrastructure to accommodate people with disabilities.

Inclusive urban design is the cornerstone of equitable cities, ensuring that public spaces, buildings, and infrastructure are accessible to all residents, regardless of their abilities or disabilities. This section delves into the vital realm of inclusive urban design, emphasizing the significance of accessible public spaces and buildings for people with disabilities. By prioritizing universal design principles and promoting accessibility, cities create environments where everyone can participate fully in social, economic, and cultural activities, fostering a sense of belonging and community for all residents.

8.2.1 Accessible Public Spaces: Welcoming Everyone

Accessible public spaces are fundamental to an inclusive urban environment. Cities are integrating features such as ramps, elevators, and tactile paving into parks, squares, and recreational areas, ensuring that individuals with mobility challenges can navigate these spaces independently. Seating areas with adequate back support, designated paths for wheelchairs, and sensory gardens are designed to provide sensory experiences for individuals with different abilities. By creating public spaces that are universally accessible, cities encourage social interactions, outdoor activities, and community gatherings for everyone, fostering a sense of belonging and well-being.

8.2.2 Inclusive Buildings: Beyond Compliance

Inclusive buildings go beyond mere compliance with accessibility standards; they prioritize the needs and experiences of all occupants. Buildings are incorporating features such as wide doorways, low countertops, and accessible restrooms to accommodate individuals with mobility challenges. Tactile signage and auditory cues are integrated to aid individuals with visual impairments. Sensory rooms and quiet spaces are designed to cater to individuals with sensory sensitivities. Inclusive buildings also consider the needs of individuals with neurodiverse conditions, ensuring that the environment is conducive to their well-being. By embracing universal design principles, cities create buildings where everyone can live, work, and thrive comfortably.

8.2.3 Accessible Infrastructure: Seamless Mobility for All

Accessible infrastructure encompasses transportation systems, sidewalks, and roadways designed to accommodate individuals with disabilities. Cities are investing in low-floor buses equipped with ramps, audible announcements, and designated seating areas. Sidewalks are leveled, well-maintained, and equipped with tactile indicators, ensuring safe mobility for individuals with visual impairments. Crosswalks are equipped with audible signals, enabling pedestrians to navigate intersections independently. Accessible infrastructure not only promotes mobility but also enhances the overall safety and independence of individuals with disabilities, allowing them to participate fully in urban life.

8.2.4 Community Engagement: Empowering Voices

Community engagement is at the heart of inclusive urban design. Cities are actively involving individuals with disabilities and advocacy organizations in the planning and decision-making processes. Public consultations, workshops, and focus groups provide opportunities for residents to voice their needs and preferences. Additionally, cities are collaborating with disability organizations to conduct accessibility audits, identifying areas for improvement and implementing necessary changes. By empowering the voices of individuals with disabilities, cities create environments that are not only accessible but also responsive to the diverse needs of their residents, fostering a sense of community and mutual respect.

In the subsequent sections, our exploration will extend to cultural inclusivity, social engagement programs, and the integration of diverse perspectives into urban policies, painting a comprehensive portrait of cities that prioritize accessible public spaces, inclusive design, and community engagement, promising a future where everyone can participate fully in the social fabric of the city.

Section 8.3: Community Engagement Initiatives

At the heart of vibrant and cohesive communities lie community engagement initiatives that empower residents to actively participate in shaping their neighborhoods. This section delves into the dynamic world of community-driven projects and participatory planning initiatives, highlighting their transformative impact on urban landscapes. By involving residents in decision-making processes, cities nurture a sense of ownership and pride, fostering social cohesion and strengthening the bonds that tie communities together.

8.3.1 Participatory Planning: Empowering Local Voices

Participatory planning initiatives bring together residents, local authorities, and urban planners to collaboratively envision the future of their neighborhoods. Through community workshops, town hall meetings, and interactive planning sessions, residents share their ideas, aspirations, and concerns. Urban planners incorporate this invaluable local knowledge into the planning process, ensuring that projects align with the genuine needs and desires of the community. By empowering residents to actively contribute to the decision-making process, participatory planning initiatives foster a sense of ownership and collective responsibility, transforming neighborhoods into thriving, inclusive spaces.

8.3.2 Community-Driven Projects: From Vision to Reality

Community-driven projects empower residents to initiate and lead transformative initiatives within their neighborhoods. These projects can range from creating community gardens and public art installations to organizing cultural festivals and educational workshops. By providing funding, resources, and technical support, cities enable residents to turn their creative ideas into tangible projects that enhance the quality of life for everyone. Community-driven projects not only beautify neighborhoods but also foster social connections and a sense of pride among residents. By encouraging grassroots initiatives, cities create environments where residents actively contribute to the vibrancy and identity of their communities.

8.3.3 Digital Platforms and Civic Tech: Connecting Communities

Digital platforms and civic tech solutions play a pivotal role in enhancing community engagement. Online platforms, mobile apps, and social media channels provide avenues for residents to share their opinions, report issues, and collaborate on projects. Civic tech solutions, such as interactive mapping tools and data visualization platforms, enable residents to explore urban data and participate in data-driven decision-making processes. By leveraging digital technologies, cities create inclusive spaces where residents, regardless of their physical presence, can actively engage in discussions, share feedback, and collaborate on initiatives, fostering a sense of belonging and unity among community members.

8.3.4 Neighborhood Assemblies: Strengthening Social Fabric

Neighborhood assemblies serve as forums where residents gather to discuss local issues, propose ideas, and collectively make decisions. These assemblies provide a platform for open dialogue, enabling residents to voice their concerns, share knowledge, and build consensus on important matters. Local authorities, community leaders, and experts often participate, facilitating informed discussions and collaborative problem-solving. Neighborhood assemblies strengthen the social fabric of communities by promoting transparency, trust, and mutual understanding among residents. By fostering direct communication and active participation, cities create resilient and cohesive neighborhoods where residents actively contribute to the well-being of their communities.

Chapter 9: Economic Sustainability and Innovation Hubs

Section 9.1: Innovation Districts and Tech Parks

Innovation districts and technology parks stand as beacons of economic growth, fostering collaboration between businesses, startups, research institutions, and the local community. This section delves into the concept of innovation districts and technology parks, exploring how these hubs drive economic prosperity and innovation. By creating dynamic ecosystems that facilitate knowledge exchange, research, and entrepreneurship, cities pave the way for economic sustainability and technological advancement.

9.1.1 Innovation Districts: Catalysts of Creativity

Innovation districts are urban areas intentionally designed to bring together researchers, entrepreneurs, and businesses, fostering creativity and innovation. These districts often host research institutions, universities, startups, and established companies. By providing shared spaces, networking opportunities, and access to funding, innovation districts facilitate the cross-pollination of ideas and the rapid development of new technologies. Collaborative environments within innovation districts accelerate the pace of innovation, attracting talent and investments that contribute significantly to local and global economies.

9.1.2 Technology Parks: Hubs of Technological Excellence

Technology parks are dedicated zones specifically designed to house technology-related industries and research centers. These parks offer state-of-the-art infrastructure, research facilities, and business support services. Technology parks serve as magnets for technology-driven companies, providing a conducive environment for research, development, and commercialization of cutting-edge technologies. By clustering like-minded businesses and research institutions, technology parks create synergies that promote innovation, enhance competitiveness, and drive economic growth within the region.

9.1.3 Community Engagement in Innovation Hubs: Bridging Gaps

Community engagement is integral to the success of innovation districts and technology parks. These hubs often initiate outreach programs, workshops, and mentorship opportunities that involve the local community. By integrating schools, community centers, and cultural institutions into the fabric of innovation hubs, cities foster a sense of inclusivity. Collaboration with local schools and universities ensures that the benefits of innovation and technology reach aspiring students, creating a talent pipeline for the future. By bridging the gap between innovation hubs and the broader community, cities strengthen social bonds and promote equitable access to economic opportunities.

In the subsequent sections, our exploration will extend to startup ecosystems, sustainable economic models, and the integration of technology in urban management, painting a comprehensive portrait of cities that prioritize economic sustainability, innovation, and community engagement, promising a future where economic growth is inclusive and sustainable.

Section 9.2: Startup Ecosystems and Entrepreneurship

The heartbeat of innovation, startup ecosystems are pivotal in driving economic growth and technological advancement. This section delves into the development of startup ecosystems, exploring the role of incubators, accelerators, and funding opportunities in supporting entrepreneurs. By nurturing a culture of innovation, cities empower entrepreneurs,

119

catalyzing the creation of groundbreaking solutions and fostering economic resilience.

9.2.1 Incubators: Cultivating Innovative Ideas

Incubators provide aspiring entrepreneurs with a supportive environment, mentorship, and resources necessary to transform ideas into viable businesses. These hubs of creativity often focus on specific industries, nurturing startups through the critical early stages of development. By offering shared office spaces, access to experienced mentors, and networking opportunities, incubators create fertile grounds for innovation. Successful incubated startups not only contribute to the local economy but also inspire the next generation of entrepreneurs.

9.2.2 Accelerators: Fast-Tracking Growth

Accelerators play a pivotal role in accelerating the growth of startups. These programs offer intensive mentoring, seed funding, and networking opportunities over a fixed period, typically a few months. In exchange for equity, startups receive invaluable guidance, exposure to investors, and the chance to refine their business models. Accelerators provide startups with the resources and expertise needed to scale rapidly, bringing innovative products and services to the market. By nurturing high-potential startups, accelerators enhance the city's reputation as a hub of innovation and entrepreneurship.

9.2.3 Funding Opportunities: Sowing the Seeds of Innovation

Access to funding is fundamental for the growth of startups. Cities are actively facilitating funding opportunities, connecting entrepreneurs with angel investors, venture capitalists, and government grants. These financial resources enable startups to develop prototypes, conduct market research, and expand their operations. By fostering an ecosystem where startups can secure funding, cities encourage entrepreneurship, job creation, and economic dynamism. Successful startups not only generate revenue but also attract talent and investments, contributing significantly to the city's economic sustainability.

In the subsequent sections, our exploration will extend to sustainable economic models, innovation in urban planning, and the integration of technology in economic development, painting a comprehensive portrait of cities that prioritize economic sustainability, innovation, and entrepreneurship, promising a future where startups thrive and contribute to the city's prosperity.

Section 9.3: Sustainable Economic Models

Sustainable economic models are the cornerstone of resilient and prosperous cities, balancing economic growth with environmental and social considerations. This section delves into innovative approaches, such as the circular economy and social entrepreneurship, which promote economic prosperity while addressing pressing environmental and social challenges. By redefining economic paradigms and encouraging ethical business practices, cities pave the way for a future where economic development is harmonized with social equity and environmental stewardship.

9.3.1 The Circular Economy: Closing the Loop

The circular economy is a transformative economic model that emphasizes minimizing waste, reusing products, and recycling materials to create a closed-loop system. In the circular economy, products and materials are designed for longevity and easy disassembly. Through recycling and remanufacturing processes, materials are reintegrated into the production cycle, reducing the demand for raw resources. Cities embracing the circular economy reduce landfill waste, conserve natural resources, and lower carbon emissions. By fostering a culture of sustainability and circularity, cities not only promote environmental stewardship but also create economic opportunities in the recycling and repurposing industries.

9.3.2 Social Entrepreneurship: Business for Good

Social entrepreneurship merges business acumen with social and environmental objectives, aiming to address societal challenges while generating revenue. Social entrepreneurs develop innovative solutions to pressing problems, often focusing on issues such as poverty, education, healthcare, and environmental conservation. These enterprises prioritize social impact, dedicating a portion of their profits to support charitable initiatives and community development projects. By harnessing the power of entrepreneurship for social good, cities promote inclusivity, reduce social inequalities, and create sustainable solutions to complex challenges. Social entrepreneurship not only empowers communities but also inspires a new generation of socially conscious business leaders.

9.3.3 Collaborative Consumption: Sharing Economy

Collaborative consumption, often referred to as the sharing economy, transforms the way individuals access goods and services. Peer-to-peer platforms facilitate the sharing, renting, or exchanging of resources, including transportation, accommodation, and household items. This economic model promotes resource efficiency, reduces overconsumption, and fosters a sense of community. By embracing collaborative consumption, cities lower the overall demand for new products, leading to reduced production-related emissions and resource depletion. Additionally, the sharing economy enhances social connections, encouraging trust and collaboration among residents.

In the subsequent sections, our exploration will extend to innovation in urban planning, the integration of technology in economic development, and the intersection of economic sustainability with social inclusivity, painting a comprehensive portrait of cities that prioritize sustainable economic models, innovation, and social entrepreneurship, promising a future where economic prosperity is synonymous with environmental conservation and social well-being.

Chapter 10: Resilience and Climate Change Adaptation

Section 10.1: Flood-Resistant Infrastructure

Explore innovative flood-resistant infrastructure designs, including floating buildings and flood barriers, enhancing cities' resilience against rising sea levels and extreme weather events.

In the face of rising sea levels and the increasing frequency of extreme weather events, cities are pioneering innovative flood-resistant infrastructure designs. This section delves into the forefront of engineering and architecture, exploring solutions such as floating buildings and flood barriers that enhance cities' resilience against the devastating impacts of floods. By embracing cutting-edge technologies and sustainable design principles, cities are fortifying their foundations to withstand the challenges posed by climate change, ensuring the safety and well-being of their residents.

10.1.1 Floating Buildings: Navigating Rising Waters

Floating buildings, also known as amphibious architecture, are innovative structures designed to rise and fall with water levels. These buildings are equipped with buoyant foundations, allowing them to float during floods and return to their original positions once the water recedes. Floating homes, offices, and public spaces not only provide a solution to flooding but also offer a unique living experience. Cities are integrating floating buildings into waterfront developments, transforming vulnerable flood-prone areas into resilient, adaptive communities. By embracing this revolutionary approach, cities ensure that residents can continue their lives even in the face of periodic flooding, fostering a sense of security and stability.

10.1.2 Flood Barriers: Guardians of Urban Landscapes

Flood barriers are robust structures strategically placed along riverbanks and coastlines to shield cities from inundation. These barriers can be temporary or permanent, deploying advanced engineering techniques to withstand the force of floodwaters. Flood barriers often incorporate elements such as retractable gates, levees, and seawalls, creating a formidable defense against rising sea levels and storm surges. By investing in sophisticated flood barrier systems, cities protect vital infrastructure, residential areas, and cultural landmarks from the destructive power of floods. These barriers not only shield cities from immediate damage but also safeguard the long-term heritage and economic assets of the community.

10.1.3 Green Infrastructure: Nature's Resilient Response

Green infrastructure, including wetlands, green roofs, and permeable pavements, acts as a natural buffer against flooding. Wetlands, in particular, serve as natural sponges, absorbing excess water during heavy rains and storm surges. Green roofs and permeable pavements allow rainwater to be absorbed into the ground, reducing surface runoff. Cities are strategically integrating green spaces and natural habitats into their urban landscapes, enhancing the city's capacity to absorb and manage excess water. By harnessing the power of nature, cities promote biodiversity, improve water quality, and bolster their resilience against floods, creating sustainable and ecologically balanced urban environments.

In the subsequent sections, our exploration will extend to climate-responsive urban planning, disaster preparedness, and the intersection of resilience with community engagement, painting a comprehensive portrait of cities that prioritize adaptation and resilience, promising a future where communities thrive in the face of climate challenges.

Section 10.2: Climate-Responsive Urban Planning

Climate-responsive urban planning is the cornerstone of building cities that can adapt to the changing climate. This section delves into innovative strategies such as green zoning, climate-sensitive building codes, and urban forestry. By integrating these approaches, cities can mitigate the impact of climate change, ensuring a sustainable and resilient future.

10.2.1 Green Zoning: Nurturing Urban Greenery

Green zoning involves the strategic allocation of green spaces within urban areas. Parks, gardens, and green corridors are meticulously planned to absorb excess rainwater, reduce heat island effects, and enhance biodiversity. Green zones act as lungs for the city, filtering pollutants, providing habitats for wildlife, and offering recreational spaces for residents. By preserving and expanding green zones, cities create resilient urban environments, fostering ecological balance and enhancing the overall quality of life for their residents.

10.2.2 Climate-Sensitive Building Codes: Designing for the Future

Climate-sensitive building codes mandate construction practices that consider the local climate and potential climate change impacts. Buildings are designed to withstand extreme weather events, conserve energy, and minimize environmental impact. These codes often include specifications for insulation, roofing materials, and energy-efficient HVAC systems. By enforcing climate-sensitive building codes, cities enhance the durability of their infrastructure, reduce energy consumption, and decrease greenhouse gas emissions, laying the foundation for a sustainable urban future.

10.2.3 Urban Forestry: Nature's Air Purifiers

Urban forestry involves the strategic planting and maintenance of trees in urban areas. Trees act as natural air purifiers, absorbing carbon dioxide and releasing oxygen. Additionally, they provide shade, reducing the urban heat island effect, and help manage stormwater runoff. Urban forests enhance the aesthetic appeal of cities, promote biodiversity, and improve air quality. By investing in urban forestry initiatives, cities create resilient green landscapes, mitigating the impact of climate change and fostering a healthier environment for their residents.

Section 10.3: Disaster Preparedness and Community Resilience

Disaster preparedness and community resilience are essential components of climate change adaptation. This section explores initiatives such as early warning systems, community engagement, and effective response plans. By involving communities in disaster preparedness and building resilient social networks, cities empower their residents to face challenges collectively.

10.3.1 Early Warning Systems: Timely Alerts for Safety

Early warning systems utilize advanced technologies to detect and predict natural disasters such as floods, hurricanes, and wildfires. These systems provide real-time alerts, giving residents and authorities crucial time to prepare and evacuate if necessary. By investing in early warning technologies, cities enhance their disaster preparedness, saving lives and minimizing property damage. These systems also promote public awareness, educating residents about potential risks and appropriate safety measures.

10.3.2 Community Engagement: Empowering Residents

Community engagement initiatives involve residents in disaster preparedness efforts. Workshops, drills, and awareness campaigns inform residents about evacuation routes, emergency shelters, and first-aid procedures. Additionally, communities are encouraged to develop local resilience plans, identifying vulnerable populations and resources that can be mobilized during emergencies. By empowering residents to actively participate in disaster preparedness, cities create a strong network of support and solidarity, ensuring that no one is left behind during times of crisis.

10.3.3 Effective Response Plans: Coordinated Crisis Management

Effective response plans are meticulously crafted strategies that outline the roles and responsibilities of various stakeholders during and after a disaster. These plans include coordination between emergency services, local authorities, and non-governmental organizations. By conducting regular drills and simulations, cities ensure that responders are well-prepared to handle diverse scenarios. Effective response plans prioritize the safety and well-being of residents, guiding cities in their efforts to swiftly recover and rebuild after a disaster.

In the subsequent sections, our exploration will extend to future trends and speculations, including underwater cities, space-based habitats, AI-driven urban management, and the intersection of technology with urban resilience, painting a comprehensive portrait of cities that are not only prepared for the challenges of today but also for the uncertainties of tomorrow.

Chapter 11: Future Trends and Speculations

Section 11.1: Underwater Cities and Marine Habitats

As humanity explores innovative solutions for the future, the concept of underwater cities and marine habitats has captured the imagination of urban planners and architects. This section delves into the speculative realm of submerged living spaces, exploring potential technologies and challenges associated with human habitation beneath the ocean's surface. By envisioning underwater cities, humanity contemplates a future where sustainable, self-sufficient communities thrive in harmony with the marine environment.

11.1.1 Submerged Living: Architecture Beneath the Waves

Underwater cities challenge traditional notions of architecture, requiring structures that can withstand immense water pressure, resist corrosion, and provide a safe and habitable environment for residents. Architects and engineers are exploring innovative materials and construction techniques, drawing inspiration from marine life and ecosystems. Submerged living spaces may incorporate transparent materials, allowing natural light to penetrate the depths and creating a surreal, ethereal ambiance. By embracing advanced engineering, underwater cities can offer residents a unique and awe-inspiring living experience, fostering a deep connection with the oceanic world.

11.1.2 Ecological Balance: Coexisting with Marine Life

Creating underwater habitats necessitates a delicate balance between human needs and marine ecosystems. Architects and biologists collaborate to design structures that do not disrupt the natural habitat, ensuring minimal impact on marine life. Artificial reefs, integrated into the architecture, provide shelter for fish and other marine organisms. Additionally, sustainable waste management systems prevent pollution of the surrounding ocean. By prioritizing ecological balance, underwater cities can become harmonious extensions of the marine environment, promoting biodiversity and preserving the delicate underwater ecosystems.

Section 11.2: Space-Based Habitats and Extraterrestrial Colonies

The exploration of space has opened the door to visionary concepts of space-based habitats and colonies on other planets. This section delves into the speculative realm of extraterrestrial living, examining the role of space exploration and technology in humanity's future beyond Earth. By envisioning space-based habitats, humanity contemplates a future where interplanetary communities thrive, pushing the boundaries of human potential and knowledge.

11.2.1 Space Habitats: Microcosms in the Cosmos

Space habitats are enclosed environments designed to sustain human life in the harsh conditions of space. These habitats may orbit celestial bodies or float freely in space, creating self-contained ecosystems. Advanced life support systems, hydroponic gardens, and recycling technologies ensure a continuous supply of oxygen, water, and food. Space habitats serve as research platforms, enabling scientists to study human behavior, physiology, and psychology in isolation. By developing self-sufficient space habitats, humanity pioneers the colonization of space, paving the way for future interplanetary exploration and habitation.

11.2.2 Extraterrestrial Colonies: Humanity Beyond Earth

Extraterrestrial colonies represent the pinnacle of human ambition, signifying our expansion beyond Earth's confines. Lunar bases, Mars colonies, and habitats on moons of distant planets are among the envisioned extraterrestrial settlements. Colonists in these outposts would face challenges such as radiation exposure, extreme temperatures, and limited resources. However, advances in 3D printing, robotics, and in-situ resource utilization (ISRU) technologies offer promising solutions. Colonies would harness local resources, such as regolith on the Moon and Martian soil, to construct habitats and produce essential supplies. By establishing extraterrestrial colonies, humanity not only ensures the survival of our species but also unlocks the mysteries of the cosmos, ushering in a new era of interplanetary civilization.

Section 11.3: AI-Driven Urban Management and Virtual Cities

The integration of artificial intelligence (AI) in urban management has transformative potential. This section explores the speculative realm of AI-driven urban management and virtual cities, envisioning a future where AI systems optimize urban designs and policies before implementation. By harnessing the power of AI, cities can enhance efficiency, sustainability, and resident well-being, ushering in an era of intelligent urban environments.

11.3.1 AI-Driven Urban Planning: Optimizing Cityscapes

AI-driven urban planning involves sophisticated algorithms that analyze vast datasets, predicting trends and simulating urban scenarios. Planners use AI models to optimize traffic flow, energy consumption, waste management, and public services. These systems provide real-time insights, enabling cities to respond dynamically to changing demands. AI-driven urban planning ensures that cities are adaptive, efficient, and responsive to the needs of their residents. By harnessing predictive analytics and machine learning, cities can anticipate challenges and proactively implement solutions, creating smart, resilient urban environments.

11.3.2 Virtual Cities: Simulating Urban Futures

Virtual cities are digital simulations of real urban environments, created through advanced modeling and AI algorithms. These virtual replicas allow planners, architects, and policymakers to test urban designs and policies in a risk-free digital space. Virtual cities facilitate collaborative planning, enabling stakeholders to visualize proposed changes and assess their impact. By immersing themselves in virtual environments, residents can actively participate in the decision-making process, providing valuable feedback and insights. Virtual cities serve as laboratories for innovation, fostering creativity and experimentation. By integrating AI-driven simulations into urban planning, cities can explore multiple futures, identifying the most sustainable and desirable paths forward.

Chapter 12: Ethical Considerations in Future Cities

Section 12.1: Privacy and Surveillance in Urban Environments

As cities become more connected and technologically advanced, the ethical implications of data privacy and surveillance practices come to the forefront. This section explores the delicate balance between utilizing technology for urban efficiency and safeguarding individual privacy rights. By examining current practices, ethical frameworks, and potential future scenarios, cities can navigate the complexities of privacy and surveillance in an increasingly digital landscape.

12.1.1 The Digital Panopticon: Balancing Security and Privacy

The advent of smart cities has introduced sophisticated surveillance systems, including facial recognition, biometric scanning, and real-time location tracking. While these technologies enhance security and assist law enforcement, they raise concerns about individual privacy and civil liberties. Striking a balance between public safety and personal privacy requires transparent policies, strict regulations, and robust oversight mechanisms. Cities are exploring ethical guidelines that protect citizens' rights while ensuring the effective use of surveillance

139

technologies. Additionally, educating the public about the scope and limitations of these systems fosters awareness and promotes responsible usage, creating an informed citizenry.

12.1.2 Data Ownership and Consent: Empowering Citizens

In the digital age, data has become a valuable commodity, driving urban decision-making and shaping services. Ethical considerations surrounding data ownership, consent, and transparency are paramount. Cities are adopting policies that prioritize citizen consent and empower individuals to control their data. Transparent data usage policies, clear consent mechanisms, and accessible data management platforms allow residents to make informed choices about their personal information. By prioritizing data ethics, cities build trust with their residents, ensuring that data-driven innovations are respectful of individual privacy rights.

12.1.3 Accountability and Oversight: Ensuring Ethical Practices

Accountability and oversight mechanisms are essential to maintain ethical standards in surveillance practices. Independent audits, oversight boards, and regular assessments of surveillance technologies ensure compliance with ethical guidelines and legal regulations. Cities are establishing collaborative frameworks involving government agencies, civil society organizations, and technology experts to assess the ethical implications of surveillance technologies. Ethical impact assessments, akin to environmental impact assessments, are becoming standard practice before deploying new surveillance systems. By fostering accountability and transparency, cities uphold ethical standards, protecting the rights and dignity of their residents.

In the subsequent sections, our exploration will extend to ethical considerations in artificial intelligence, environmental justice, and equitable access to technology, painting a comprehensive portrait of cities that prioritize ethical principles, resident well-being, and social equity.

Section 12.2: Ethical AI and Algorithmic Decision-Making

As artificial intelligence (AI) continues to play a significant role in urban management, ethical considerations in AI development and algorithmic decision-making become crucial. This section delves into the ethical implications of AI, addressing topics such as bias, transparency, and accountability. By ensuring ethical AI practices, cities can harness the power of technology while upholding fairness and social equity.

12.2.1 Bias in AI: Addressing Algorithmic Prejudice

AI algorithms can inadvertently perpetuate societal biases present in training data. Biased algorithms can lead to discriminatory outcomes, affecting marginalized communities disproportionately. Ethical AI development involves identifying and mitigating biases in algorithms. Researchers and developers are exploring techniques such as fairness-aware machine learning, where algorithms are designed to minimize disparate impacts. Additionally, transparency in AI algorithms allows external scrutiny, ensuring fairness and preventing unintended discrimination. By proactively addressing bias, cities create AI systems that are equitable and just.

12.2.2 Transparency and Explainability: Demystifying AI Decisions

Transparency in AI refers to making the decision-making process of algorithms understandable to non-experts. Ethical AI systems provide clear explanations for their decisions, enabling users and affected individuals to understand how conclusions are reached. Explainable AI (XAI) technologies, such as interpretable machine learning models, enable transparency in complex algorithms. Transparent AI systems enhance accountability, allowing citizens to question decisions and hold institutions responsible. By embracing transparency and explainability, cities foster trust in AI technologies, ensuring that residents have insight into the systems shaping their lives.

12.2.3 Accountability and Oversight: Ethical Governance of AI

Accountability in AI refers to the clear assignment of responsibility for AI systems and their outcomes. Ethical governance frameworks define roles and responsibilities for developers, regulators, and users of AI technologies. Oversight mechanisms, including ethics boards and regulatory agencies, assess the ethical implications of AI deployments. Cities are adopting ethical AI principles and guidelines, involving multi-stakeholder collaborations to establish best practices. Continuous monitoring and evaluation of AI systems ensure they align with ethical standards. By implementing robust accountability measures, cities ensure that AI technologies serve the public good and contribute to societal progress.

Section 12.3: Environmental Justice and Equitable Access to Technology

Environmental justice and equitable access to technology are fundamental ethical considerations in urban development. This section explores the intersection of environmental sustainability, social equity, and technological access. By prioritizing environmental justice and digital inclusion, cities create inclusive environments where all residents have equal opportunities and access to resources.

12.3.1 Environmental Justice: Bridging the Green Divide

Environmental justice advocates for fair treatment and meaningful involvement of all people, regardless of race, income, or socio-economic status, concerning the development, implementation, and enforcement of environmental laws, regulations, and policies. Cities are addressing environmental injustices by investing in green infrastructure, clean energy, and sustainable transportation in underserved communities. By closing the green divide, cities ensure that marginalized neighborhoods have access to clean air, water, and green spaces, promoting both environmental and social equity.

12.3.2 Digital Inclusion: Bridging the Digital Divide

Digital inclusion aims to provide all residents, regardless of their socio-economic status, with access to information and communication technologies. Cities are implementing initiatives such as public Wi-Fi networks, digital literacy programs, and affordable internet access to bridge the digital divide. Educational institutions and community centers serve as hubs for digital learning, enabling residents to acquire essential digital skills. By ensuring digital inclusion, cities empower residents to access online education, job opportunities, and essential services, fostering social equity and economic mobility.

Section 12.4: Citizen Engagement and Participatory Governance

Citizen engagement and participatory governance are integral to building inclusive, democratic, and responsive urban communities. This section delves into the ethical imperative of involving residents in decision-making processes, ensuring that diverse voices shape urban policies. By fostering active citizen participation, cities strengthen democratic values, enhance transparency, and promote social cohesion.

12.4.1 Inclusive Decision-Making: Empowering Communities

Inclusive decision-making processes prioritize diverse perspectives, ensuring that the voices of all residents are heard and respected. Cities are implementing town hall meetings, citizen assemblies, and online platforms to solicit public input on key issues. Inclusive decision-making involves marginalized communities traditionally left out of policy discussions. City leaders are working to dismantle barriers to participation, such as language barriers and lack of access to information, enabling all residents to engage meaningfully. By empowering communities to co-create their urban environments, cities build a sense of ownership and pride among residents, fostering a shared vision for the future.

12.4.2 Digital Democracy: Enhancing Access to Civic Participation

Digital democracy leverages technology to enhance citizen engagement and streamline participatory processes. Cities are adopting online voting platforms, interactive decision-making apps, and virtual town halls to enable residents to participate in governance from the comfort of their homes. These digital tools provide real-time feedback to policymakers, allowing them to respond swiftly to residents' needs. Additionally, digital democracy promotes transparency by making government actions and decisions accessible to the public. By embracing digital platforms, cities enhance civic participation, ensuring that technology bridges the gap between citizens and their representatives.

Section 12.5: Cultural Inclusivity and Diversity in Urban Policies

Cultural inclusivity and diversity in urban policies are essential for fostering vibrant, tolerant, and harmonious communities. This section explores the ethical imperatives of recognizing cultural diversity, protecting cultural heritage, and celebrating different identities within cities. By embracing cultural inclusivity, cities strengthen social fabric, promote intercultural dialogue, and create a rich tapestry of urban life.

12.5.1 Preserving Cultural Heritage: Safeguarding Identity

Preserving cultural heritage involves protecting historical sites, traditions, and languages unique to different communities. Cities are enacting policies to conserve cultural landmarks, museums, and artistic expressions. Additionally, cultural education programs in schools and public spaces celebrate diverse heritages, fostering mutual respect and understanding. By safeguarding cultural identity, cities ensure that residents take pride in their heritage, promoting a sense of belonging and cohesion.

12.5.2 Inclusive Events and Festivals: Celebrating Diversity

Inclusive events and festivals provide platforms for communities to showcase their traditions, art, music, and cuisine. Cities are organizing multicultural festivals, art exhibitions, and heritage fairs that celebrate the richness of diverse cultures. Inclusive events promote cross-cultural interactions, breaking down barriers and prejudices. Furthermore, cities are supporting grassroots cultural initiatives, enabling artists and cultural entrepreneurs to thrive. By celebrating diversity, cities create vibrant public spaces where residents appreciate each other's cultures, fostering social harmony and unity.

In the subsequent sections, our exploration will extend to the integration of technology into cultural preservation, social engagement programs, and the role of arts in urban regeneration, painting a comprehensive portrait of cities that prioritize cultural inclusivity, social equity, and ethical governance.

Section 12.4: Citizen Engagement and Participatory Governance

Citizen engagement and participatory governance are integral to building inclusive, democratic, and responsive urban communities. This section delves into the ethical imperative of involving residents in decision-making processes, ensuring that diverse voices shape urban policies. By fostering active citizen participation, cities strengthen democratic values, enhance transparency, and promote social cohesion.

12.4.1 Inclusive Decision-Making: Empowering Communities

Inclusive decision-making processes prioritize diverse perspectives, ensuring that the voices of all residents are heard and respected. Cities are implementing town hall meetings, citizen assemblies, and online platforms to solicit public input on key issues. Inclusive decision-making involves marginalized communities traditionally left out of policy discussions. City leaders are working to dismantle barriers to participation, such as language barriers and lack of access to information, enabling all residents to engage meaningfully. By empowering communities to co-create their urban environments, cities build a sense of ownership and pride among residents, fostering a shared vision for the future.

12.4.2 Digital Democracy: Enhancing Access to Civic Participation

Digital democracy leverages technology to enhance citizen engagement and streamline participatory processes. Cities are adopting online voting platforms, interactive decision-making apps, and virtual town halls to enable residents to participate in governance from the comfort of their homes. These digital tools provide real-time feedback to policymakers, allowing them to respond swiftly to residents' needs. Additionally, digital democracy promotes transparency by making government actions and decisions accessible to the public. By embracing digital platforms, cities enhance civic participation, ensuring that technology bridges the gap between citizens and their representatives.

Section 12.5: Cultural Inclusivity and Diversity in Urban Policies

Cultural inclusivity and diversity in urban policies are essential for fostering vibrant, tolerant, and harmonious communities. This section explores the ethical imperatives of recognizing cultural diversity, protecting cultural heritage, and celebrating different identities within cities. By embracing cultural inclusivity, cities strengthen social fabric, promote intercultural dialogue, and create a rich tapestry of urban life.

12.5.1 Preserving Cultural Heritage: Safeguarding Identity

Preserving cultural heritage involves protecting historical sites, traditions, and languages unique to different communities. Cities are enacting policies to conserve cultural landmarks, museums, and artistic expressions. Additionally, cultural education programs in schools and public spaces celebrate diverse heritages, fostering mutual respect and understanding. By safeguarding cultural identity, cities ensure that residents take pride in their heritage, promoting a sense of belonging and cohesion.

12.5.2 Inclusive Events and Festivals: Celebrating Diversity

Inclusive events and festivals provide platforms for communities to showcase their traditions, art, music, and cuisine. Cities are organizing multicultural festivals, art exhibitions, and heritage fairs that celebrate the richness of diverse cultures. Inclusive events promote cross-cultural interactions, breaking down barriers and prejudices. Furthermore, cities are supporting grassroots cultural initiatives, enabling artists and cultural entrepreneurs to thrive. By celebrating diversity, cities create vibrant public spaces where residents appreciate each other's cultures, fostering social harmony and unity.

Section 12.6: Integration of Technology into Cultural Preservation

The integration of technology into cultural preservation offers innovative ways to protect and promote cultural heritage in urban environments. This section explores how cities leverage digital tools, virtual reality, and augmented reality to preserve historical sites, artifacts, and traditions. By embracing technological advancements, cities can bridge the gap between the past and the future, ensuring that cultural heritage remains vibrant and accessible to future generations.

12.6.1 Digital Archives and Virtual Museums: Preserving Cultural Artifacts

Digital archives and virtual museums enable cities to digitize historical artifacts, documents, and artworks, making them accessible to a global audience. Advanced imaging technologies and digital curation methods ensure the preservation of delicate items while creating immersive online experiences. Cities are collaborating with museums, libraries, and universities to create extensive online repositories, allowing researchers and the public to explore cultural heritage from their devices. By digitizing cultural artifacts, cities ensure their preservation for future generations while fostering knowledge sharing and academic research.

12.6.2 Augmented Reality Heritage Trails: Interactive Cultural Experiences

Augmented reality (AR) heritage trails transform urban spaces into interactive cultural experiences. Using AR apps on smartphones or AR glasses, residents and tourists can explore historical sites, landmarks, and cultural narratives overlaid with digital information. Cities are developing AR heritage trails that blend the physical and digital worlds, providing users with immersive storytelling experiences. These interactive trails engage users with historical events, architectural marvels, and cultural traditions, enhancing their appreciation for the city's heritage. By integrating technology into cultural preservation, cities create dynamic and educational experiences, ensuring that cultural heritage remains a vital part of urban life.

Section 12.7: Social Engagement Programs and Arts in Urban Regeneration

Social engagement programs and the arts play a pivotal role in urban regeneration, revitalizing communities, and enhancing social cohesion. This section explores the ethical significance of investing in social engagement initiatives, supporting local artists, and integrating arts into urban planning. By prioritizing social and cultural enrichment, cities create inclusive environments where creativity thrives, fostering a sense of pride and unity among residents.

12.7.1 Community Arts Projects: Empowering Local Creativity

Community arts projects empower local artists and residents to collaborate on creative endeavors. Cities are supporting mural painting, sculpture installations, and public art exhibitions that reflect the cultural diversity of neighborhoods. Community engagement in art projects promotes a sense of ownership and pride among residents, fostering community identity. Additionally, these projects create vibrant public spaces that attract visitors and stimulate local economies. By investing in community arts, cities empower residents to shape their environments creatively, enhancing the overall quality of life.

12.7.2 Arts-Based Urban Interventions: Transforming Public Spaces

Arts-based urban interventions involve transforming neglected or blighted areas into vibrant cultural hubs. Cities are repurposing abandoned buildings, alleys, and underpasses into art galleries, theaters, and creative spaces. These interventions not only rejuvenate urban landscapes but also provide platforms for artists and performers to showcase their talents. Arts-based interventions encourage community gatherings, cultural events, and artistic collaborations, fostering a sense of belonging among residents. By embracing arts-based urban regeneration, cities create aesthetically pleasing environments that inspire creativity and social interaction, revitalizing neighborhoods and promoting social equity.

Section 12.8: AI-Driven Urban Management and Virtual Cities

The integration of artificial intelligence (AI) into urban management and the concept of virtual cities present novel ethical challenges and opportunities. This section examines how AI-driven simulations and virtual environments can enhance urban planning, optimize resource allocation, and foster innovation. By embracing these technologies ethically, cities can pave the way for more sustainable, efficient, and inclusive urban futures.

12.8.1 AI-Powered Urban Simulations: Shaping Future Landscapes

AI-powered urban simulations utilize complex algorithms and data analytics to model various scenarios for urban development. Cities are leveraging these simulations to assess the impact of new infrastructures, zoning regulations, and transportation systems. By simulating different scenarios, urban planners can make informed decisions that maximize efficiency, reduce environmental impact, and enhance quality of life for residents. Ethical considerations in this context involve ensuring the transparency of simulation methodologies and the responsible use of predictive data. By involving diverse stakeholders in the simulation process, cities uphold democratic principles and create urban plans that reflect the needs and aspirations of their communities.

12.8.2 Virtual Cities: Testing Grounds for Innovation

Virtual cities, digital replicas of urban environments, serve as testing grounds for innovative ideas and urban experiments. These virtual spaces allow architects, urban planners, and policymakers to visualize and analyze the impact of proposed changes in a controlled digital environment. Virtual cities facilitate public engagement, enabling residents to explore and comment on planned developments virtually. Ethical considerations include ensuring the accessibility of virtual platforms to all residents, regardless of their technological proficiency. Cities are investing in user-friendly interfaces and interactive tutorials to empower residents to participate in the virtual planning process. By embracing virtual cities ethically, urban development becomes a collaborative endeavor, incorporating diverse perspectives and expertise.

In the subsequent sections, our exploration will extend to topics such as sustainable transportation innovations, advancements in healthcare and public health, and the ethical implications of human augmentation technologies. These discussions will paint a comprehensive portrait of cities that prioritize ethical principles, technological innovation, and resident well-being.

Conclusion

In the boundless expanse of our cities, where millions of lives intertwine, a future of unparalleled promise and sustainable harmony beckons. This exploration into the realms of urban transformation, sustainable innovation, and inclusive community design has illuminated the path toward the cities of tomorrow. Our journey through the pages of this book has been a testament to the collective ingenuity, resilience, and determination of humanity to craft environments that resonate with life, energy, and endless possibilities.

As we conclude this odyssey, it is evident that the future of cities rests in the hands of visionaries, architects, engineers, urban planners, and, most importantly, the communities they serve. The tapestry of our cities is woven from the threads of eco-friendly architecture, renewable energy solutions, intelligent infrastructure, and inclusive community engagement. Each chapter, section, and subsection has contributed a vital hue to this vibrant tapestry, emphasizing the essential elements that shape cities into thriving, sustainable, and resilient hubs of human endeavor.

From the visionary concepts of vertical forests and smart grids to the practical implementations of safe housing and efficient waste management, we have witnessed the transformational power of innovative ideas and their impact on urban landscapes. The emphasis on ethical considerations, social inclusion, and cultural diversity has underscored the imperative of building cities that are not just structurally sound but also morally grounded, embracing every individual and their unique contributions.

Our exploration has not merely been an intellectual exercise; it has been a call to action. It resonates with the urgency of the challenges we face - climate change, rapid urbanization, social disparities - and beckons us to respond with creativity, compassion, and unwavering resolve. The chapters on ethical considerations remind us that every decision made today reverberates through the generations, urging us to make choices that safeguard our planet and honor the diversity of human experience.

In the chapters on urban infrastructure, we encountered the challenges of our times - the need for robust road networks, clean water supply, and wastewater management. We recognized the significance of earthquake-resistant buildings, safe living spaces, and resilient businesses. These challenges, though daunting, are not insurmountable. They are invitations for innovation, opportunities for collaboration, and catalysts for transformation.

As the final pages of this book turn, they mark not an end, but a new beginning. The insights gathered within these chapters serve as blueprints for the architects of the future, guiding them toward the creation of cities that are not only sustainable but also nurturing, not only efficient but also compassionate. The dialogue initiated here must echo in boardrooms and community centers, in city halls and classrooms, inspiring initiatives that transform cities from concrete jungles into vibrant, green, and inclusive havens for all.

In this concluding chapter, we extend a profound gratitude to the visionaries, the pioneers, the thinkers, and the doers who are shaping the cities of tomorrow. We celebrate the communities that inspire change, the innovators who challenge the status quo, and the leaders who envision a future where cities are not just habitats but vibrant, living organisms that breathe life into the dreams of every citizen.

The future of our cities is not a distant vision; it is a tapestry being woven today, in the decisions we make, in the collaborations we forge, and in the values we uphold. Let this book be a catalyst for that future, a source of inspiration, knowledge, and above all, a call to action. Together, let us embark on this transformative journey, hand in hand, and build cities that stand as testaments to the human spirit's boundless capacity to innovate, adapt, and flourish. The future of our cities is in our hands, and it is a future of limitless possibilities.